RARY

return

VICTORY
★ IN THE ★
PACIFIC

VICTORY
★ IN THE ★
PACIFIC

PEARL HARBOR TO THE FALL OF OKINAWA

Karen Farrington

ARCTURUS

Arcturus Publishing Limited
26/27 Bickels Yard
151–153 Bermondsey Street
London SE1 3HA

Published in association with

foulsham

W. Foulsham & Co. Ltd,
The Publishing House, Bennetts Close, Cippenham,
Slough, Berkshire SL1 5AP, England

ISBN 0-572-03129-7

This edition printed in 2005

Copyright © 2005 Arcturus Publishing Limited

All rights reserved

The Copyright Act prohibits (subject to certain very limited exceptions)
the making of copies of any copyright work or of a substantial part of
such a work, including the making of copies by photocopying or similar
process. Written permission to make a copy or copies must therefore
normally be obtained from the publisher in advance. It is advisable also
to consult the publisher if in any doubt as to the legality of any copying
which is to be undertaken.

British Library Cataloguing-in-Publication Data: a catalogue record for this
book is available from the British Library

Printed in China

Edited by Paul Whittle
Book design by Beatriz Waller
Layout by Steve West
Maps by Roger Hutchins

Picture Credits:
Cover Photo © Imperial War Museum, London
Imperial War Museum
pp. 8, 35, 45, 46, 47, 48, 56, 62, 64, 68, 70, 72, 78, 81, 83, 97, 98, 99, 101,
102, 105, 1067, 109, 112, 114, 119, 120, 123, 126, 128, 130, 131, 132, 135,
136, 138
ITN Archive
pp. 9, 16, 17, 29, 30, 44, 49, 51, 60, 65, 74, 79, 80, 90
United States Naval Historical Foundation
pp. 11, 13, 19, 20, 23, 25, 26, 31, 32, 34, 36, 38, 41, 42, 52, 85, 92, 93, 94
Hulton Getty
pp. 15, 54, 57, 86, 95, 96, 111, 116, 118, 124, 127, 133, 141

940.5426
Ω 62358L

CONTENTS

THE PACIFIC THEATRE 1941-1945

CHINA

USSR

Maximum Extent of
Japanese-held Territory

GREATER ASIAN
CO-PROSPERITY
SPHERE

PACIFIC

Okinawa

Iwo Jima

BURMA

Hong Kong

Bataan

Guam

Yap

NEW GUINEA

Guadalcanal

AUSTRALIA

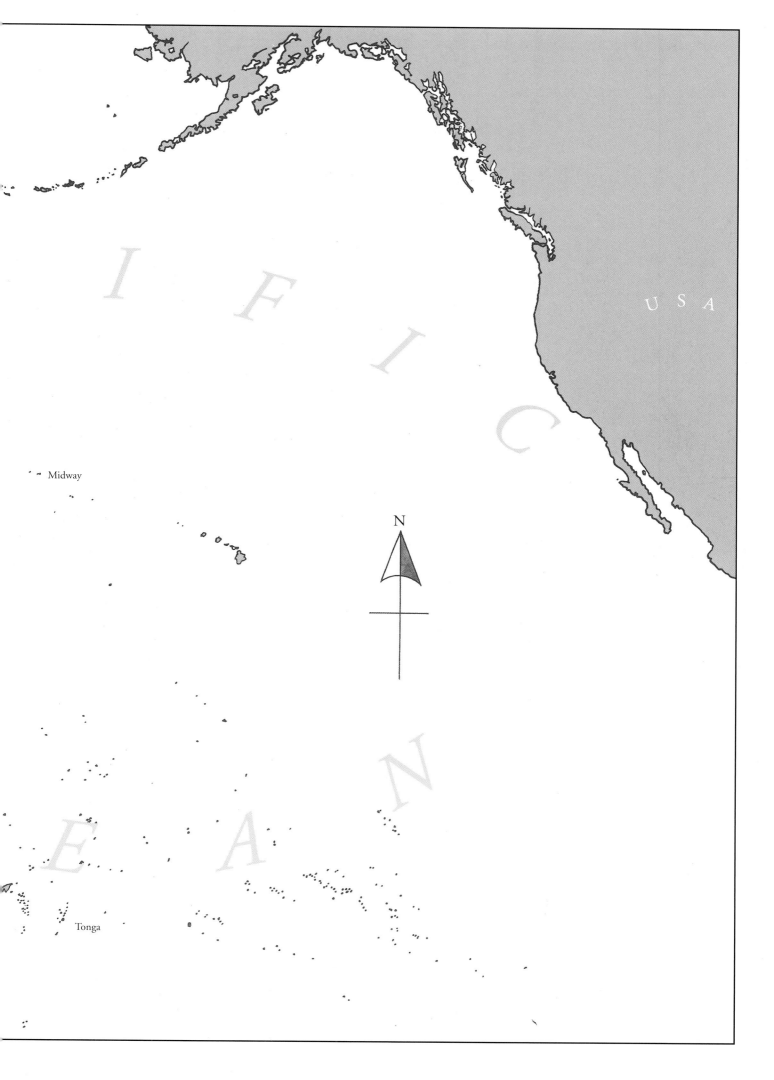

Out Of A Clear Blue Sky: The Attack on Pearl Harbor

*'December 7... a day
that will live in infamy'*

US PRESIDENT FRANKLIN D ROOSEVELT

On 7 December 1941, to the echo of the war cry 'Tora, Tora, Tora!', the Imperial Japanese Navy launched an attack against the American fleet anchored in the shelter of Pearl Harbor, Hawaii. The shock at Pearl Harbor itself and throughout the United States was palpable. Diplomacy in the region had hit a rough patch but no one expected anything of this magnitude.

Pearl Harbor is usually portrayed as the ultimate in surprise attacks – the surprise attacker's surprise attack, so to speak – yet to anyone familiar with the superpower politics then being played out in the Pacific, the attack was less surprising. Japan had been shaping up towards some serious expansion for quite a time. Long frustrated by what they saw as American and British circumvention of their grand designs for empire, Japan's war leaders also believed that the long drawn-out European war had sapped the will of Britain and her immediate allies to defend their possessions in the East. While they were otherwise engaged in hostilities, Japan's ruling military class believed, Japanese hegemony could be established over these imperial possessions without difficulty and that it was manifestly right to do so.

It is curious, however, that the war leaders of this small but fervently militaristic Pacific nation chose to take on just about the largest power in the world when it could not possibly hope to compete on terms. Japan's population was half that of its new-found foe, while its industrial

capacity was a fraction of that achieved in America at the time. It is true that the US was far from a war footing – although gearing up for conflict had already begun – and that had the attack on Pearl Harbor been executed as planned the largest part of the US Navy would have been annihilated, leaving Japan master of the seas. Yet Japan did not achieve the stunning victory at Pearl Harbor it had hoped for and had no further hammer blow to deliver. The best it could hope for was a compromise, never a victory. America's recovery from this initial set back was always assured – indeed it went on to illustrate the capacity to wage war simultaneously in the Pacific and Europe – and that bleak prospect from Japan's perspective was

apparent to at least some of its commanders. Admiral Isoroku Yamamoto, the schoolmaster's son, Harvard graduate and architect of the Pearl Harbor attack, was acutely aware of the predicament Japan now faced. With heavy heart he said 'I fear we have only awakened a sleeping giant and his reaction will be terrible.'

American losses were undeniably colossal at Pearl Harbor. The battleships *Arizona* and *Oklahoma* were sunk as were the target ship *Utah* and the minelayer *Oglala*. Lying above the water line although seriously damaged were the battleships *California*, *West Virginia* and *Nevada* along with *Tennessee*, *Maryland* and *Pennsylvania*. The cruisers *Helena*, *Raleigh* and *Honolulu* were likewise

It's War

British newspapers annnounce the Japanese surprise attack on Pearl Harbor, 7 December 1941 (above); the Japanese naval commander who led the attack, Admiral Isoroku Yamamoto (facing page).

damaged along with the destroyers *Cassin*, *Downes* and *Shaw*. At the nearby airfield 164 aircraft were destroyed and a further 128 were damaged.

For their part the Japanese losses were slight. Just a few aircraft were lost out of 183 that took part in the initial raid, along with five midget submarines. (American sailors were slow to respond as their ammunition and guns were locked away as per required safety standards.) More Japanese fliers were lost in a second attack due to the hazards of flying in the heavy smoke palls that now rose above Pearl Harbor, making a total of 29 lost crews. Sixty-four men were dead or missing (one was taken prisoner), compared with American losses amounting to 2,403 servicemen and civilians. A further 48 Hawaiian civilians died.

A declaration of war made by the Japanese to pre-empt the military action by 30 minutes was lost in translation and only became known much later. After their return from Pearl Harbor, some Japanese pilots involved in the attack heard that no declaration of war had been made before the first bomb dropped and felt stripped of an immense victory, tainted by dishonour. Yamamoto too felt there was no pride in attacking a sleeping enemy. He also believed Japan had handed America its emotive battle cry: 'Remember Pearl Harbor'. Yet this sense of unease was not generally felt. The Japanese celebrated on the streets of Tokyo, believing the conflict would be swift and the rewards great.

But while the Japanese populace celebrated their success and Americans seethed about apparent Japanese treachery, the underlying failure of the Japanese mission was not yet discernible. The US carrier fleet had sailed and was not among

USS *Arizona*

The forward superstructure of the USS Arizona, burning during the attack on Pearl Harbor. To the right of the picture are the ship's undamaged boat cranes, and her mainmast.

Memorial

The USS Arizona *memorial at Oahu in Hawaii, erected amidships over the sunken ship herself.*

the Pearl Harbor victims. American ships, obligingly parked in lines for Japanese pilots as they homed in, were easy targets, but oil installations at Pearl Harbor were still either intact or repairable as were the dockside facilities. Without them the US would have been compelled to withdraw to the American mainland. If that had happened the Japanese navy, the third biggest in the world behind the US and Britain, would have reigned supreme for a considerable time. As it was the American navy retained a foothold in the Pacific that would prove vital in future actions.

American pride was badly mauled, however. The loss of life was huge and the injuries sustained by those who survived were appalling. Thirty sets of brothers were dead and three US families lost all three sons in that two-hour attack. Men were still being pulled alive from the steel hulls of the half-sunk ships 36 hours after

the Japanese planes vanished into the clear Pacific skies.

The lack of intelligence that left the American ships like rows of sitting ducks became a cause for internal investigation and no small amount of fury. Debate about who was to blame and why has cropped up innumerable times in the subsequent decades. From a distance of more than 60 years it seems that although some Japanese codes had been broken, America was still operating with peace-time values and possessed no sense of urgency about monitoring its uppity neighbour. Communications between Washington and Pearl Harbor were patchy, although word that Japan was going to launch an attack imminently had been circulating in Washington early that December; indeed, rumour had abounded about Japanese intentions for most of the year. However, there was no indication the target was going to be Pearl Harbor, while the Japanese commander Vice-Admiral Chuichi Nagumo kept a strict radio silence as he advanced 3,000 miles in ten days from his home base via a discreet route to a distance of 275 miles (440 km) north of Hawaii, yielding no clues as to his intentions and his destination.

The idea that President Franklin D. Roosevelt knew about the impending catastrophe but chose to do nothing in order that America would join the ongoing international conflict under a united banner appears to hold no water. He was not by nature a cynical man. Nor is there a single document to support the theory that he sacrificed the forces at Pearl Harbor to satisfy a lust or need for war. The difficulty that plagued the Americans in the run-up to war was that Pearl Harbor was never mentioned. Singapore seemed a far more likely target for Japanese forces when viewing the politics of the day, not to mention the geography of the region, and what the Japanese would stand to gain.

Torpedo Planes

attack 'Battleship Row' in this photograph taken from a Japanese aircraft. Torpedo drop splashes and running tracks are visible at left and centre. White smoke in the distance is from Hickam Field. Grey smoke in the centre middle distance is from the torpedoed USS Helena.

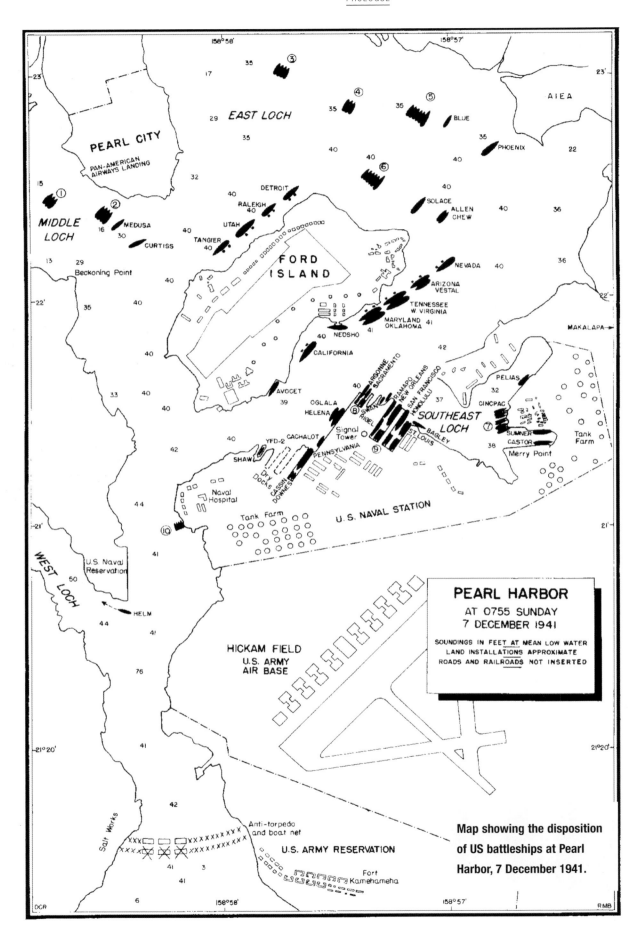

Map showing the disposition of US battleships at Pearl Harbor, 7 December 1941.

However, prior to Pearl Harbor Roosevelt was undeniably uncomfortable about the power struggle underway around the world and the way that America stood apart from it. His desire to fight Germany alongside Britain had been tempered for diplomatic purposes by the unpopularity of war among Americans, many of whom highly valued the country's isolationist stance. Thus the attack at Pearl Harbor did achieve some of his ambitions. Addressing the House of Congress on the day after Pearl Harbor, Roosevelt said: 'Yesterday, December 7, 1941 – a date which will live in infamy – the United States of America was suddenly and deliberately attacked.' The subsequent American declaration of war was a foregone conclusion.

After the conflict General Hideki Tojo, the prime minister of Japan, revealed that the decision to go to war with the United States was taken at an Imperial Conference held in Tokyo on 1 December 1941. According to Tojo, Emperor Hirohito, the country's divine ruler, did not utter a single word in response.

Tension had been building between Japan and the West for more than a decade. Controls on the size of its navy imposed by America and Britain caused considerable ire, which was compounded by the economic constraints brought about by the Wall Street crash in 1929. Frustrated by international diplomacy which appeared to work against her interests, Japan left the League of Nations as early as 1933.

America's protectionist policies and immigration laws were taken like slaps in the face by the burgeoning Japanese nation. It had argued that Britain had its sphere of influence in (non-European) Asia, America had its highly protected

trade revenues from South America and Japan merely sought to ensure that the Pacific was the area in which it would dominate and prosper. Britain and America would hear nothing of it.

A quest to make Japan into a pseudo Western power was being continually rebutted. Now Japan wanted to leave the west in its wake and planned an empire that would resolve some of its natural disadvantages, especially a shortage of fuel. When America responded with oil and iron sanctions against Japan for its overseas adventures into Chinese territory after 1931 and then French IndoChina a

It's War

President Franklin D. Roosevelt signs the declaration of war on Japan which, less than four years later, would lead to the dropping of the atom bomb on the Japanese home islands.

decade later, believing that could bring the increasingly rogue nation to heel, the proud and prepared Japanese army felt war was the sole alternative for the nation's survival. The army enjoyed rampant power at the time. Manpower was no problem as every young man was conscripted into one of the services. Ironically, General Tojo was chosen as prime minister to help rein in the ambitions of the army, but even his powerful personality was insufficient to unite the riven factions that existed in Japan, particularly between army and navy.

In fact the Japanese sought to place puppet governments in the lands it had occupied rather than superimpose imperialist rule from Tokyo. After nine years the war with the Chinese had reached something of a stalemate by 1940. Had the conflict not escalated to embrace Britain and America there was a chance that Japan, devoting all its resources to that arena, would have won against China, wiping out the future opportunity for Chinese communists and Mao Tse Tung.

A statement from Emperor Hirohito was issued on 8 December 1941 to explain to the Japanese why their country had ended up at war:

'. . . *To cultivate friendship among nations and to enjoy prosperity in common with all nations, has always been the guiding principle of Our Empire's foreign policy. It has been truly unavoidable and far from Our wishes that Our Empire has been brought to cross swords with America and Britain. More than four years have passed since China, failing to comprehend the true intentions of Our Empire and recklessly courting trouble, disturbed the peace of East Asia and compelled Our Empire to take up arms. Although there*

Manchuria

Japanese soldiers take a break during their invasion of Manchuria, known as the 'Manchurian Incident', in 1931.

has been re-established the National Government of China with which Japan had effected neighbourly intercourse and cooperation, the regime which has survived at Chungking, central China, relying upon American and British protection, still continues its fratricidal opposition. Eager for the realization of their inordinate ambition to dominate the orient, both America and Britain, giving support to the Chungking regime, have aggravated the disturbances in East Asia. . . They have obstructed by every means our peaceful commerce and finally resorted to a direct severance of economic relations, menacing gravely the existence of Our Empire. Patiently we have waited and long have we endured in the hope that Our Government might retrieve the situation in peace. But Our adversaries showing not the least spirit of conciliation have unduly delayed a settlement and in the meantime they have intensified the economic and political pressure to compel Our Empire to submission. . . . The situation being such as it is Our Empire for its existence and self defence has no other recourse but to appeal to arms and to crush every obstacle in its path.'

The statement was republished on the eighth day of each month in every newspaper in Japan until September 1945.

On the March

The Japanese invasion of China lasted from 1937 until they were finally ousted in 1945, after the Allied victory.

CHAPTER ONE

The Coral Sea and Midway

Had the Battle of Midway gone the other way, America's Pacific war would have been considerably prolonged.

For Winston Churchill, the news of America's entry into the war was all good and he was flooded with a sense of relief and well-being. On 9 February 1941 he had appealed for American help with the words 'give us the tools and we will finish the job'. In reality Britain was already under great strain – as was Churchill himself – and victory was far from assured. His nightmare scenario was that Japan would attack British and perhaps Dutch interests in the Pacific region and still the US would stay out of the conflict. He strongly felt that 'the great crescent' of colonial possessions in the Far East – between India, Burma and Singapore – belonged firmly inside the boundaries of the British empire. Churchill was aware that American intervention would secure a triumph, given its immense industrial output and seemingly inexhaustible supply of men. He embarked for a meeting with Roosevelt in Washington on 12 December with his tail up in the knowledge that, with diplomatic issues simplified and mostly resolved, America was in the war 'up to the neck and in to the death'. They had declared war on Japan almost in unison and together Britain and the States would tackle the militarist menace of the east.

Since 27 September 1940 Japan had been in the Tripartite Agreement with Hitler and Mussolini, an agreement which now bound the fate of those three countries. It ruled that the signatories recognized each other's plans for expansion and would come to the aid of one another if attacked. Hitler made his second catastrophic mistake of 1941 when he declared war on the US as a perverse gesture of support for Japan. (His first immense error of judgement was to invade Russia in June that year.)

Japan continued to make itself aggressively busy at various Pacific pit stops during the ensuing weeks while America took a few moments to analyse its position. Until some of the resources lost at Pearl Harbor were replaced it would be severely restricted in its activities, fighting defensive or delaying actions rather than going on the offensive. And despite a seemingly ceaseless string of Japanese success stories, the Allied Combined Chiefs of Staff decided the war against Germany had to be given priority. Roosevelt said: 'Germany is the greater enemy; once we've defeated Germany we shall be able to deal with Japan.' Once that important decision was made it was never up for negotiation. Britain's anxieties about the fate of India, a cash cow for the empire, were noted by the Americans, but the defence of the subcontinent was not made a priority. The Americans, never great sympathizers with imperial aims other than their own, believed pure self interest was driving Britain's concerns. Six US field armies were sent to Europe compared to three – the Sixth, the Eighth and the Tenth – that were destined for the Pacific.

US Resolve

There was, however, a strong resolve in the US navy that matters were in hand in the Pacific to combat the spiralling influence of the Japanese. There was a part to be played by Allied forces too, particularly the Australians and New Zealanders in the arena. However, the weight of numbers came out of the United States of America and consequently it was largely left to call the shots.

American commanders were Fleet Admiral Ernest King, who made it his business to funnel as much military hardware into the Pacific as possible despite the priority given to Europe and the Atlantic, Admiral Chester Nimitz and General Douglas MacArthur, Commander in Chief of the South West Pacific Area, based in Melbourne, Australia.

In common with the armed services of other nations involved in the conflicts, there was competition between the US army and navy for territory and influence. In the vast waters of the Pacific there were no great swathes of land to conquer as there were in Europe and little need for heavily-armed ground forces, putting the army at an immediate disadvantage. Thus, the start of World War II as far as the Americans were concerned was very much a naval affair, with the ships complemented for the first time by carrier-borne aircraft. Only later did the emphasis switch to amphibious assault.

The Doolittle Raid

In the spring of 1942 America began to exercise its muscle with raids by planes based on aircraft carriers against the Gilbert and Marshall Islands. This inspired sufficient confidence for the Doolittle raid to take place against the Japanese mainland, the most daring exploit by the Americans in the war to that date.

On 18 April, 16 B-25 bombers from the Army Air Corps under the command of Lieutenant Colonel James Doolittle, each carrying one ton of bombs and ferried into the Pacific by the USS *Hornet*, set out for Japan, some 600 miles distant.

Later mission commander and pilot Doolittle explained the intention of the raid: 'It had three real purposes. One purpose was to give the folks at home the first good news that we'd had in World War II. It caused the Japanese to question their

Bombs Away

Lieutenant Colonel James H. Doolittle, of the US Army Air Force, wires a Japanese medal to a 500-pound bomb, shortly before his force of sixteen B-25B bombers took off for Japan on what became known as the Doolittle Raid, 18 April 1942.

warlord. And, from a tactical point of view, it caused the retention of aircraft in Japan for the defence of the home island when we had no intention of hitting them again seriously in the near future. Those planes would have been much more effective in the South Pacific where the war was going on.'

Doolittle had carved a reputation for himself by teaching aerial combat tactics during World War One. He returned to the air corps in 1940 when it seemed war was imminent, helping to convert the car manufacturing facilities in the States to military production. The science of aerial warfare had changed but Doolittle proved himself up to the challenge by embracing the task of mounting a raid on Japan. Training had been rigorous. Although the aircraft carrier was in many ways ideal for the task, the pilots had to practice take off on a ship's runway nearly half the size previously used.

Hopes that the ship could spring the planes from a point even closer to their target were dashed when the aircraft carrier unexpectedly encountered Japanese patrol boats en route. The small boats were duly sunk – but not before warnings had been radioed back about the approaching American force.

Rather than abandon the raid, it was brought forward, in the hope of pre-empting a Japanese response to the presence of the *Hornet*. The cities hit included Tokyo, Kobe and Yokohama. The intention was then to fly towards China, at war with Japan for some five years already and now benefiting from US aid. But now the pilots were wrestling with fuel shortages caused by their fast start. One of the planes came down near Vladivostock and its crew was jailed by the surprised Russians who were not yet at

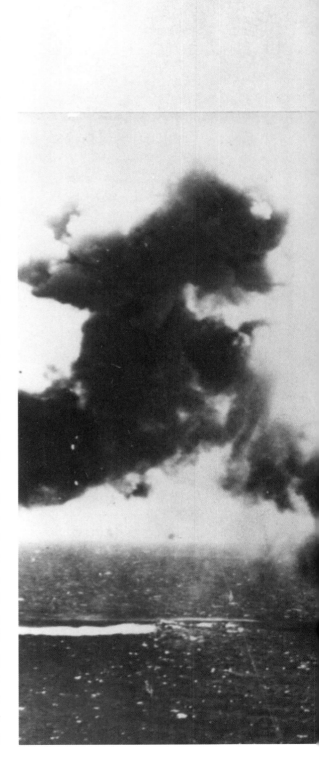

Battle of the Coral Sea

Japanese aircraft carrier Shoho *is torpedoed by US Navy carrier aircraft in the late morning of 7 May 1942, during the Battle of the Coral Sea.*

war with Japan. Two planes and eight men fell into Japanese hands. All were made prisoners of war, with three ultimately being shot. Two men drowned after their plane came down in the sea. However, a hearteningly large percentage of the crew survived, although some suffered serious injuries, among them Ted Lawson, who lost a leg. Within the year he would collaborate on a book about the raid that was quickly made into a film called *30 Seconds Over Tokyo*.

Although damage in Japan was comparatively slight the embarrassment factor for the country's high command was indeed huge as it no longer seemed bomb-proof as previously believed by the populace. No one was expecting the home islands to be hit – at least, not so soon in the conflict.

Until then the Japanese were at odds about the direction in which to channel their war efforts. One faction favoured pressing west towards Fiji and Samoa while another believed the key to success was a drive northwards into Russia. For his part, Yamamoto was insistent that the Midway Islands were the essential 'pin prick' landfalls that were pivotal to Japanese success in the war. His cause was assisted immeasurably following the Doolittle raid as a sense of urgency about the need to destroy US naval might now prevailed.

The Battle of the Coral Sea

The first stand-off between Japanese and US navies occurred at the Battle of the Coral Sea on 7 and 8 May 1942, the first of six key battles between the two. It took place in the waters that are bordered by the Solomon Islands, Papua New Guinea, Australia and, to the south, New Caledonia.

Through diligent monitoring of enemy communications, the Americans discovered a plan to capture Port Moresby, on New Guinea's south eastern coast and troublingly close to Australia. (As if to confirm their intentions, the Japanese carried out a limited number of small raids against the northern coast of Australia.)

The upshot was a long-distance confrontation between the Japanese aircraft carriers *Shokaku* and *Zuikaku*, and their assorted escort craft, and the USS *Lexington* and the USS *Yorktown*, also with support craft including some from Australia. Although the action was crucial the major craft on both sides never came closer than 70 miles to one another and were generally much further apart than that. It was carrier-borne aircraft that were key. Sea battles had never been fought like this before, with the ships failing to exchange a shot. This fact, coupled with a lack of exact intelligence on the precise whereabouts of the prize enemy targets, led to the sinking of secondary vessels in great numbers.

On 7 May 1942 Japanese spy planes reported that a carrier and a cruiser were at a certain location and a substantial force of attack planes was dispatched to deal with them. In fact, it was a US oil cargo ship and an escorting destroyer. Both were wrecked by enemy action.

In turn America dished out similar treatment to a light carrier, *Shoho*, and four cruisers. While all were targeted by a volley of bomber and fighter planes they were in fact second rate objectives. The Japanese, however, had no idea where the American planes had come from.

The following day the serious business of aircraft carrier destruction got underway. Almost simultaneously each side's planes attacked the other's water-borne

targets. If the action was to be judged in terms of winners and losers then the Japanese edged a marginal victory. The American aircraft carrier *Lexington* was torpedoed and bombed and after being abandoned by the crew she sank the same day. *Yorktown* was also badly damaged and had to withdraw. In reply American planes wreaked sufficient damage on *Shokaku* to ensure her departure for safer waters. Many more Japanese aircraft were lost than American. But benefiting from low cloud cover, the *Zuikaku* was undam-

aged. However, over-extended Japan was in no position to capitalize on these small gains and their forward movement had been halted. Its navy, although undefeated, had pulled out of a battle and that was by itself a boost for the Americans and their allies.

The Battle of Midway

A month later came the Battle of Midway and this time the result was far more clear cut in America's favour.

The Midway Islands, measuring just

Dauntless

Dauntless dive bombers from USS Hornet *approaching the already fatally-damaged Japanese heavy cruiser* Mikuma *in the third set of attacks on her, during the early afternoon of 6 June 1942.*

two square miles (5 sq km), sit squarely in the Pacific Ocean, unpopulated except for US military personnel. It was a second string naval base for the Americans in the Pacific after Pearl Harbor.

Admiral Isoroku Yamamoto, Japanese Combined Fleet Commander, had twin aims in mind when he manoeuvred his forces towards the two tiny islands. He envisaged a swift invasion to oust the incumbent Americans and gain control of a strategically vital airfield. Also, he believed Japanese action would entice US aircraft carriers into action, where they could be scuppered by a superior Japanese strike force. For good measure, he instigated a simultaneous operation to capture the Aleutian Islands, in the North Pacific off the coast of Alaska, to distract American forces.

All this he might have achieved had it not been for intelligence experts in America who had translated the guts of Japanese coded information. Far greater emphasis had been placed on the importance of eavesdropping since Pearl Harbor and resources in the form of the Combat Intelligence Office were devoted to it. Advance information paid dividends during the Battle of the Coral Sea. Now it was set to do so again as Americans watched the build up of Japanese navy ships. Cryptologists, though, were unsure of the target.

The suspicion was that Midway was the objective but no one was sure. Commander Joseph P. Rochefort, in charge of intelligence, secretly asked the base at Midway to broadcast a bogus message over the radio, claiming that its water desalination plant was out of order. Soon Japanese coded traffic revealed the target was having problems with fresh water provision. Now America was certain where the assembled enemy fleets were heading and it meant that US aircraft carriers could motor into position even before the arrival of the unsuspecting Japanese, in possession of almost every element of Yamamoto's strategy. In the American line of battle was the *Yorktown*, repaired in record time following the damage inflicted less than a month previously.

At dawn on 4 June 1942 both sides sent out spotter planes to locate the enemy. The American pilots came across the Japanese forces as expected. For their part the Japanese were concentrating on the military strength of Midway, believing – with good reason – that their Zero planes were superior to the island's American aircraft. Only later did they discover the presence of the American fleet.

Initially, everything went Japan's way. Although the airbase escaped largely unscathed the tally of hits against its aircraft by Zero fighters was immense for few losses. The Mitsubishi A6M 'Zero' fighter was the pride of the Japanese fleet, being both highly manoeuvrable and fast. When their fleet size was restricted, Japan concentrated on honing the weaponry and skills of its naval air arm. It worked in conjunction with the Aichi D3A dive bomber, known as 'Val' to the Allies, and the Nakajima B5N otherwise known as 'Kate', an attack aircraft in possession of an 18 inch torpedo or a 1,757 lb armour piercing bomb. All were ferried into position by the three carrier fleets.

Within hours the US navy and army planes had joined in both the pursuit of the Japanese planes and an attack on their carrier ships. The best conclusion that can be drawn from these first efforts by old and slow aircraft is that they disrupted preparation for a second wave of bombing by the agile Zeros.

It wasn't until 10.25 am – some four hours after the first skirmishes over Midway – that significant headway was forged by the Americans. When success came it was immediate and immense. Three squadrons of scout bombers – two from the *Enterprise* and one from the *Yorktown* – targeted the four carriers whose decks were by now busy with refuelled and fully-armed aircraft. In a matter of moments the carriers *Akagi*, *Kaga* and *Soryu* were blazing and crippled as the explosive effects delivered by the American planes were multiplied many times by the Japanese armaments aboard.

Now only *Hiryu* remained operational.

By way of reprisal 18 dive bombers escorted by six fighters from the sole surviving carrier sought out the *Yorktown* about 90 minutes later and wreaked havoc when three bombs scored direct hits. A second attack wave against the *Yorktown* mounted by the Japanese caused further damage and the listing vessel had to be abandoned. Two days later a torpedo from a Japanese submarine sent her to the bottom.

However, US carrier planes went after *Hiryu* once more and inflicted significant damage. Fires raged out of control and

Pearl Harbor Revenged

Japanese heavy cruiser Mikuma, *during the afternoon of 6 June 1942, after she had been bombed by planes from* USS Enterprise *and* Hornet.

Hiryu's crew ultimately had to jump ship. Unable to face the loss of their ship and the failure of military action, Admiral Yamaguchi and Captain Kaku committed suicide. Within a few hours Yamamoto abandoned the Midway operation, into which he had invested almost every available naval vessel, and retreated. The Japanese took two tiny islands but the cost was tremendous. The Imperial Japanese Navy lost four heavy carriers, one heavy cruiser, 100 pilots, 3,400 sailors, three carrier skippers and a carrier admiral. By way of a bonus to the Americans, the wreckage of a crashed Zero was seized and was to be scrutinised by experts seeking its weak points. American losses amounted to one carrier, a destroyer and 150 planes. The sharp edge of Japanese aggression, which until now had been as incisive as a switchblade, was at last blunted. Had the result gone a different way, America's Pacific War would have been drawn out immeasurably. With its victory at Midway America ensured that Japan could no longer dictate in the confrontations at sea, and the US was now able to draw up some agendas of her own. It was six months after Pearl Harbor and already in the battle for mastery of the seas the tide had turned in favour of America.

Norman Bel Geddes diorama, depicting the torpedoing of USS Hammann *and USS* Yorktown *by Japanese submarine* I-168, *on the afternoon of 6 June 1942, during the Battle of Midway.*

CHAPTER TWO

Guadalcanal

*'There are only three types of Marine:
those overseas, those going overseas, and
those who have been overseas.'*

MAJOR GENERAL ALEXANDER VANDEGRIFT

The largest of the Solomon Islands, some 90 miles in length and about 25 miles in width, Guadalcanal amounts to 2,500 sq miles (6,475 sq km) of typically tropical landscape that includes steep-sided volcanoes and steamy ravines. It was here that the Americans decided to mount a first offensive against the occupying Japanese forces. And it was on this jungle smothered island, home to countless millions of disease-bearing mosquitoes, that Americans got a first taste of how the rest of the war would be on landfalls in the Pacific. At Guadalcanal there was bitter fighting, a protracted campaign, heavy losses and an intransigent enemy. There began a war of attrition that reduced men from both sides into ravaged, nerve-ridden victims.

At first the job in hand seemed simple

Raid on Darwin

Oil tanks in Darwin, in Australia's Northern Territory burn following a Japanese air attack on 19 February, 1942.

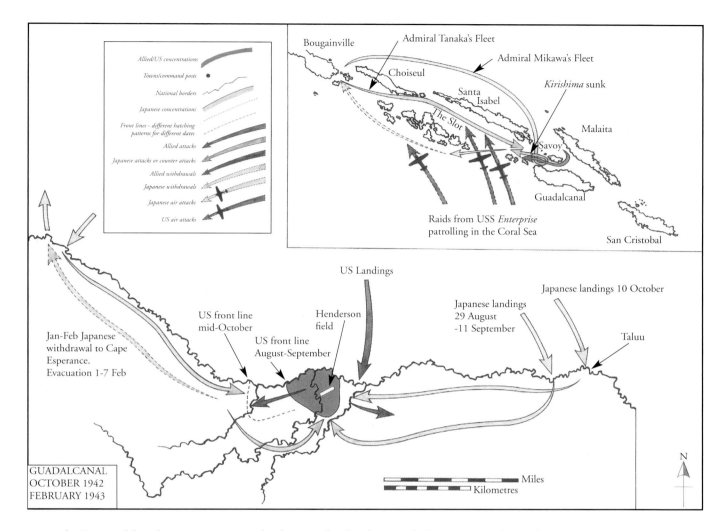

Map legend:
- Allied/US concentrations
- Towns/command posts
- National borders
- Japanese concentrations
- Front lines - different hatching patterns for different dates
- Allied attacks
- Japanese attacks or counter attacks
- Allied withdrawals
- Japanese withdrawals
- Japanese air attacks
- US air attacks

Bougainville • Admiral Tanaka's Fleet • Admiral Mikawa's Fleet • Choiseul • *Kirishima* sunk • Santa Isabel • The Slot • Malaita • Savoy • Guadalcanal • San Cristobal

Raids from USS *Enterprise* patrolling in the Coral Sea

US Landings

Japanese landings 10 October

Jan-Feb Japanese withdrawal to Cape Esperance. Evacuation 1-7 Feb

US front line mid-October

Henderson field

US front line August-September

Japanese landings 29 August -11 September

Taluu

GUADALCANAL OCTOBER 1942 FEBRUARY 1943

Miles
Kilometres

N

enough. Buoyed by the successes notched up at Midway, the Americans decided it was time for a land grab to further destabilize the Japanese forces around the region in a joint operation between the army and the navy. There was also a need to ensure Australia and New Zealand could not be severed from the US by Japanese action on the island chains of the Pacific. The Japanese had already flagged their hostile intentions towards Australia with an air raid on Darwin on 19 February 1942 by 188 aircraft. In command was Mitsui Fuchida, the man who led the flight formations at Pearl Harbor.

The results of the raid at Darwin were disastrous for Australia, not least because an early warning system had broken down. The US destroyer *Peary* was sunk in the harbour while an Australian ship, *Neptuna*, loaded with explosives, exploded killing its captain and crew. Other victims included dock workers, the post master and his family who took a direct hit and US pilots approaching the local airfield. Afterwards the Lowe report decided that 243 people had been killed and as many as 400 injured. At least some of the deaths might have been prevented if better use had been made of coast watchers' warnings about an on-coming flight of Japanese planes. It was the first and by far the most serious of more than 60 raids mounted against northern Australia during 1942 and 1943.

With the enemy building an airstrip on Guadalcanal, which would lend it dominance in that neighbourhood, this island now seemed an ideal candidate for invasion. It was intended to be a stepping stone with American forces forging forward through other islands in the Solomon strip to Papua New Guinea.

American planners were caught out, however, when the Japanese sent troops into Buna on Papua New Guinea. This substantial island sitting north of Australia's Cape York was now once again in real danger of falling into enemy hands. Papua New Guinea – specifically Port Moresby – remained a crucial target for the Japanese in their bid to secure the region and it was equally vital for the Americans and Australians to keep them out. Allied troops were diverted there and the assault on Guadalcanal by the 1st US Marine Division was temporarily delayed.

Finally on 7 August the invasion got underway – and none of the portents until then had been good. The code name Operation *Watchtower* was soon changed to Operation *Shoestring* by participants when they realized the extent of shortfalls in the budget. When Europe was given priority as a battleground it inevitably meant there would be difficulties in providing adequately for Pacific operations. Meanwhile the Allied plans to mount an amphibious landing in North Africa later in 1942 were also sucking up supplies. However, the men did get sight of the bow ramp landing craft for the first time and sampled the advantages of close air support from carrier-based aircraft.

The men earmarked for the operation were not considered battle ready. Their commanders were not expecting them to go into action until 1943. The rehearsals

Smoke and Confusion

Japanese aircraft mount another raid, this time against Australian defences at Port Moresby on Papua New Guinea.

they had conducted in Fiji before setting off for Guadalcanal were, in the words of General Archie Vandegrift, 'a complete bust'. Relations between the army and the navy, given joint responsibility for the amphibious assault, were far from cordial. It seemed the operation was dogged by mishap.

Still, on 31 July twenty-three transports and cargo ships set off from Fiji with Guadalcanal, Tulagi, an island two miles long and a few hundred yards wide, and the Santa Cruz islands on the agenda. Some 19,000 Marines were carried in 13 large transports, six cargo ships and four small high speed transports. Direct naval support included eight cruisers, 15 destroyers and five high-speed minesweepers. Further out at sea there lay three aircraft carriers, with a battleship, six cruisers, 16 destroyers and five oilers commanded by Vice Admiral Frank Jack Fletcher.

Only as the invasion unfolded did good fortune finally smile on the task force. Japanese aircraft had been grounded by poor weather and consequently the island's defence forces had no advanced warning about an invasion. When 11,000 Marines came ashore that August

Henderson Field

on Guadalcanal, photographed from a USS Saratoga plane in the latter part of August 1942, after US aircraft had begun to use the airfield. Ironbottom Sound is just out of view at the top.

Beach Blue →

1-A/A Reported →

2-A/A Positions reported →

From Above

Annotated vertical aerial photograph of Tulagi, prepared for planning purposes shortly before the island was captured by US Marines on 7-8 August 1942.
'Beach Blue' was the Marine landing area during the operation.

morning they found that, against expectation, they walked up the beach unmolested. Within 24 hours the newly constructed airfield was in American hands along with a considerable quantity of abandoned enemy equipment. The airfield was now known as Henderson Field.

At Tulagi, about 20 miles away, the defenders – a tougher breed of Japanese servicemen than those on Guadalcanal – were quicker off the mark so there was some exchange of fire, sufficient to claim the lives of 108 Americans, and the Japanese fought almost to the last man. Still, the descending Americans outnumbered the Japanese and the stars and stripes soon fluttered over the territory which became a ship's hospital for the region.

The most critical aspect of the operation was that the beaches on Guadalcanal were quickly getting clogged up with men, machinery and the necessary supplies. Marines refused to help sailors with the task, highlighting an on-going competitive conflict between the services. Higgins' boats, used to ferry cargo, as yet had no front ramp and proved difficult to off-load. The LVT tractors or 'alligators' did prove their worth in shipping supplies to land, however. The painful need for an effective post-invasion plan was sorely apparent and hard lessons learned on Guadalcanal would be used to hone the D-day landings, two years later.

Pfc James Donahue was among the Marines and he recalled his first days on Guadalcanal in a journal now published on the internet.

'The jungle is thick as hell. The Fifth regiment landed first and marched to the airport. We went straight through and then cut over to block the escape of the Japs. It took three days to go six miles. Japs took off, left surplus first day which was done away with.
'The second day was murder. All along the way were discarded packs, rifles, mess gear and everything imaginable. The second night it rained like hell and the bugs were terrible. The Second Battalion had reached the Lunga River. We had to cross four streams.
'The third day we came back. The Japs had beat us in their retreat. We took up beach defence positions. We have been bombed every day by airplanes and a submarine shells us every now and then.
'Our fox holes are four ft deep. We go out on night patrols and it is plenty rugged. We lay in the foxholes for 13 to 14 hours at a clip and keep firing at the Japs in the jungles. As yet there is no air support. The mosquitoes are very bad at night. The ants and fleas bother us continually. The planes strafed the beach today. A big naval battle ensued the

second day we were here, which resulted in our ship, the Elliot, being sunk. All of our belongings were lost.
'We raided the Jap village and now we are wearing Jap clothes. It is extremely hot. USS North Carolina sunk two cruisers and destroyers. Japs are still in the hills. We have no AA guns but use the half tracks against the Jap airplanes. Japs landed food and ammunition by parachute.
'Our Lt Colonel ambushed and bayoneted. We cleared brush from river for an expected Jap landing. The patrols are going deeper into the jungle each night. They tried to ambush us last night. We are not allowed to fire.'

The Japanese clearly had no intention of permitting a walkover. They decided the best response would be made by sea – and thus the elongated campaign for Guadalcanal became as infamous for its naval conflicts as for land-based activities.

Initially, a Japanese attempt to land more ground troops on Guadalcanal by ship from Rabaul came to grief through a torpedo from a US submarine. Waves of attacks by Japanese aircraft on the afternoon of 7 August fared little better. Their strike rate was poor – only one transport was irretrievably damaged – while their losses were enormous.

However, on 9 August the first in a series of naval battles was the one overarching Savo Island, conducted at night time. It was a sure victory for the Japanese and a humiliating breakdown in the US intelligence network.

The Japanese had no way of knowing that messages indicating their presence in the region would be lost in the system or that radar cover had failed so catastrophically that it permitted their ships to slip between two US destroyers unseen.

US Marines

come ashore on Tulagi Island, 7-8 August 1942. Fighting was fierce as, once again, the Japanese defenders fought to the last man.

Earlier that day Vice Admiral Gunichi Mikawa had spoken to his men. 'Let us go forward to certain victory in the traditional night attack of the Imperial Navy. May each one of us calmly do his utmost.'

With considerable audacity he brought his ships through The Slot, the waterway between the two strips of islands collectively known as the Solomons, and, by the light of flares dropped by carrier planes, he took his pick from a selection of targets at close range.

Three US cruisers were sunk along with one Australian in little over 20 minutes. Other ships suffered damage and the naval presence was already severely diminished following the decision by Vice Admiral Fletcher to swiftly withdraw his carrier groups from Guadalcanal. (These

were the only three US carriers available for action in the Pacific and it remained important to protect them. He had forewarned everyone that he would withdraw within 48 hours of Operation *Watchtower* in order to safeguard the ships.) Alarmed by the attack the support boats withdrew from Guadalcanal still containing supplies assigned to the invasion force but not yet unloaded, leaving the men subject to uncomfortable shortages in the weeks following. The Japanese slipped back through The Slot – also known as the New Georgia Sound – unharmed.

On the shore US Marines were cheering at the roars and flashes of battle some eight miles distant, convinced the Japanese forces were being decimated. Only the next morning did they realize it was their own ships and the men upon them that were being destroyed. With the wrecks of four ships at the ocean bottom the waters were given the new name of 'Ironbottom Sound'.

The Eastern Solomons

Before the month was out another major sea battle had been fought, this time with inconclusive results. The Battle of the Eastern Solomons involved two aircraft carriers, a light carrier, two battleships, five cruisers and 17 destroyers dispatched from the Japanese base at Rabaul in New Britain with the intention of snatching back Guadalcanal. Three American carriers came back into play or, more specifically, the aircraft launched from their decks. There were considerable aircraft and pilot losses on both sides. The Japanese carrier *Ryujo* was torpedoed along with a light carrier, a destroyer and a troop transport. The US carrier *Enterprise* took a couple of significant hits from Japanese dive bombers. With a plan to land Japanese reinforcements rendered impossible, cautious carrier captains on both sides decided to withdraw from the battle under cover of darkness. Then it was left to land-based aircraft on

Jungle Warfare

US Marines mount an attack on fiercely-defended Japanese positions, Bougainville. Japanese resistance proved to be more stubborn even than the more pessimistic forecasts.

A Break in the Fighting
US Marines rest in a jungle clearing on Guadalcanal, circa August-December 1942.

Guadalcanal – christened the Cactus Air Force comprising Marine Air Group planes and later carrier planes based at Henderson field – to harry Japanese forces who continued to make great use of The Slot under cover of darkness to land men and supplies. Agile torpedo boats were also used to disrupt the destroyer dashes that had been dubbed the Tokyo Express.

In a separate incident at the end of August the USS *Saratoga*, one of the key aircraft carriers in the region, was hit by a torpedo and forced to withdraw to Pearl Harbor for repairs. Now, in broad brush strokes, the Japanese had the advantage at sea while the Americans maintained their superiority on land.

At least some of that advantage was consolidated by a group of men known as the Seabees – official title the US Naval Construction Force – who arrived in the wake of the Marines all over the world to build roads, airstrips and scores of other construction projects.

The Seabees – motto Construimus, Batuimus (We build, We fight) – were the construction battalions that came into being after Pearl Harbor in a naval initiative headed by Rear Admiral Ben Morrell. At first men were recruited from the construction industry and the average age was 37, while some were over 60. That benchmark only decreased when voluntary enlistment was halted in December 1942.

Although they were partially trained in warfare their terms of engagement meant they were only supposed to fight to defend projects they had built. The first Seabee to receive a war decoration was Seaman 2nd class Lawrence C. Meyer who laboured to keep Henderson Field open for Allied aircraft. While he was off duty he found and repaired a Japanese machine gun. On 3 October 1942 he used it to shoot down a

Aftermath

The still-burning wreckage of a SBD scout-bomber, after it was destroyed by a Japanese air attack on Henderson Field, Guadalcanal, 1942

Japanese Zero attacking the airfield. The award was made posthumously, however, for less than two weeks after this incident he died when a fuel barge he was working on was hit by Japanese naval gunfire.

The number of Seabees who lost their lives through enemy action during World War II amounted to 272 and an additional 18 officers. Those who died through accidents numbered more than 500.

September saw a concerted effort among Japanese forces to make good the loss of Guadalcanal and literally thou-sands of men were poured on to the island. In his diary one Japanese fighter, Genjirous Inui, recorded details from this perspective. He was among men assigned to win back the airport. On September 6 his entry centres on a trek over the island and the onset of a tropical downpour. 'Having no shelters we slept in the open and Captain and all were soaked to the bone. There are many diarrhoea patients and (those with) "the smart of crotch with chaffing" (crotch rot) but the morale of the company is high.'

Soon afterwards he recalls a Japanese operation against tanks aiming to forge a path across Guadalcanal. Gunners opened fire when their targets were 500 metres (555 yards) away:

All the gunners shot tanks one after another, and many tanks were put out of action and went up in flames. They made a counterattack with their cannons and machine guns. But we fired at them at point blank range before the running tanks could find us through their small front view.
'A tank spouted black smoke from the turret, a tank was enveloped in raging flames, a tank set off an explosion in the body and a tank rushed blindly towards us, fell over a precipice on its back and flames poured from the tank. We destroyed ten tanks of 14 and four retreated into the jungle. The enemy rained down tons of trench mortar shells on our heads. They destroyed one of our guns.'

However, as 14 September dawned the failure of their considerable efforts on Bloody Ridge was starkly apparent:

The attack that was carried out full of confidence seems to be a failure. Enemy planes are already taking off safely in the morning. How mortifying! We buried our guns in the sands of the position and went ahead to the gathering point. We had the last ration of rice cut down . . . for breakfast and we had nothing for lunch.
Throughout the Americans made full advantage of the defensive points they had dug into while the Japanese were compelled to carry out an offensive with the wrong tactical guidelines. These are words typical of an address delivered by a high-ranking officer before an attack to assembled men:

It's the time to offer your life for his majesty the emperor. The flower of Japanese infantrymen is in the bayonet-charge. This is what the enemy soldiers are most afraid of. The strong point of the enemy is superiority of firepower. But it will be able to do nothing in the night and in the jungle. When all-out-attack begins, break through the enemy's defences without delay. Recapture our bitterest airfield. Rout, stab, kill and exterminate the enemy before daybreak. We are sure of the ultimate victory of the Imperial Army.'

The flaws in the Japanese battle plans were obvious from the outset. While bayonet charging did indeed terrify the Americans, they did had the weaponry to deal with it. The Japanese had to reconsider their tactics if they were to reap any significant rewards.

At sea the US had another set of problems to deal with, including the loss of another carrier, *Wasp*, to a submarine torpedo on 15 September. Now Vice Admiral William 'Bull' Halsey took charge of sea-borne operations, marking a more aggressive and successful era for the navy in the region.

On 13 October Japanese ships cratered the airstrip from the comparative safety of the Slot. Fuel stocks were set on fire and a multitude of aircraft were destroyed. Bombers were compelled to pull back to Australia for a time. However, it was much easier to supply planes and men in the Solomons from Australia than it was from the home islands of Japan.

Japanese losses continued to mount and compared unfavourably with limited numbers of casualties among the Marines — although each death was deeply felt. In his journal Donahue refers to two ambushes that ended with American fatalities:

A lot of the men were sleeping in their fox-holes as a result of working parties during the day and patrols at night. Some of these men were caught unaware by the Japs who crossed the Lunga River. Cpl K was stabbed by a Jap officer with his sabre right through his face. He then raised his sword and came down on the sleeping Cpl. The blow almost severed his leg. It hit him right on the knee bone. K was very powerful and built like a barrel. By this time EDJ, a Frenchman, had woken and attempted to shoot him, but his safety was on and all he could do was parry the Jap's next blow at him. EDJ's hand was cut badly. The Jap officer figured it was too hot for him and started to back away. C., who was about 20ft away, shot him. The next day C got his sword.

On a different occasion guerrilla tactics by the Japanese caused difficulties.

The Jap is a vicious fighting machine. A Marine patrol the other day met another patrol, which ambushed them. They were Japs with Marine helmets and uniforms. Eight Marines were killed, two Japs killed. They are sly . . . Japanese are experts on camouflage.

The US forces were not only fighting for their survival but were also formed into daily working parties to keep the airfield open and operational, among other essential tasks. At first food was basic and somewhat scarce, mail from home was the sole highlight and playing cards was the only recreation.

When US-held territory had extended a little, men bathed in the Lunga river and washed their clothes in it too. The joy of splashing in the fresh running water was occasionally punctured when the body of a dead Japanese soldier floated by.

In the battle of Santa Cruz, fought between US and Japanese carrier forces on 26 October, some 100 Nippon aircraft were shot down compared with just 74 lost by the Americans. However, it was judged a victory by the Japanese for their fighters succeeded in sinking the US carrier *Hornet*.

Even as late as 30 November the Imperial Japanese Navy was scoring victories against America. The battle of Tassafaronga occurred when five US

cruisers and six destroyers ambushed a Japanese force using the Slot to deliver supplies to Guadalcanal. However, a swift response to the opening salvoes delivered by the US soon gave the Japanese the upper hand. A torpedo attack sank an American cruiser and badly damaged three others while just one Japanese destroyer was bagged in reply. Yet the see-saw war was almost won by now, with land-based American troops in command.

In December the 1st Marine Corps was finally relieved. Vandegrift wryly observed that there were only three kinds of Marines, those that are overseas, those that have been overseas and those that are going overseas.

He was awarded the Medal of Honor by President Roosevelt for 'outstanding and heroic accomplishment' while he lead the American forces on Guadalcanal between 7 August and 9 December. For the same period Roosevelt awarded the Presidential Unit Citation to the 1st

Battle of the Santa Cruz Islands, October 1942

A Japanese 'Val' bomber trails smoke as it dives toward USS Hornet, *26 October 1942. This plane struck the ship's stack and then her flight deck. The lower aircraft is a 'Kate' shipboard attack plane.*

a Japanese bullet there were five wiped out by disease.

Nor was the fighting in the form of set metal. US fighters faced a sharp learning curve when it came to the guerrilla-style tactics employed by the Japanese, who frequently waited until their prey was within 50 ft before opening fire from camouflaged positions.

Americans were cutting their teeth on jungle warfare and were frequently exposed to danger through inadvertent tactical blunders. Units that failed to follow text-book instructions as far as rearguards, flank defences and general caution were at the mercy of the Japanese.

At times the Americans were operating 'in the dark', without the benefit of inside information. Commanders poised to pitch their men into action on Guadalcanal were even making plans

Raising the Colours

on Guadalcanal after the initial landings in August 1942 by 1st US Marine Corps. The officer second from right is probably Major General Alexander Vandegrift, CO of 1st Marines.

Marine Division for 'outstanding gallantry'. The award embraced other elements of the Armed Forces that battled alongside the 1st Marines Division.

There were some common factors throughout the fighting for Guadalcanal. The threat of disease – sometimes exacerbated by a lack of water – was ever present. Malaria and Dengue Fever were as debilitating to the fighting men as enemy action and for every one that fell to

without accurate maps, since the intelligence on Guadalcanal and its defensive positions was generally poor. On one occasion Americans attacked a Japanese defensive point believing it housed just 100 men armed with 10 heavy weapons. In fact there were more than 500 men in position with something like 50 weapons and they managed to hold off five American battalions for a month.

There were golden moments when the

reading of Japanese navy ciphers helped furnish the Americans with essential information. In addition, there was another vital link in intelligence gathering. The Coast Watching Organisation had personnel scattered about the Pacific island monitoring Japanese activity.

The CWO:
Watching the Australian Coast

The Coast Watching Organisation was formed in 1919 when it involved volunteer civilians reporting unusual or suspicious events occurring off the Australian coastline. With the onset of the Second World War and Japanese muscle-flexing, the service assumed new relevance. Coast watchers stayed in at-risk territories after the rest of the local population was evacuated and were joined by planters and other local officials. When the Japanese troops invaded, they hid behind enemy lines and radioed whatever information they could glean back to base. It might be naval or aircraft movements – helping to provide an air raid early warning system in some cases. Despite the obvious hazards the coast watchers remained unpaid volunteers although some were awarded military rank to prevent them from being shot as spies if they were captured.

Admiral Nimitz valued highly the work carried out by the coast watchers and declared as much when he said: 'The coast watchers saved Guadalcanal and Guadalcanal saved the Pacific.'

Eric Feldt, the man who headed the coast watchers, wrote about their exploits after the war. 'In Papua, New Guinea and the Solomons most civilians were evacuated. Many coast watchers, however, decided to remain and continue their

reporting. They were still civilians, were unpaid and had no provision for their families. Their only hope of surival appeared to be in the reconquest of the country by our forces, which was problematical in the dark days of 1942. Theirs was a very special type of courage.'

Ultimately the Coast Watch Organisation was absorbed by the Allied Intelligence Bureau.

By 4 January 1943 the bitter reality had become obvious even to the blinkered eyes of the Japanese high command. Those Japanese servicemen that remained on Guadalcanal were on starvation rations, prey to innumerable diseases and, crucially, were incapable of mounting another offensive. For eight days Japanese destroyers slipped along The Slot to pick up 11,000 men, with a defiant rearguard action fought to prevent attacks by US troops.

By 6 February, when Guadalcanal was declared secure, American casualties killed and wounded amounted to 6,000 out of a total of 60,000 men involved in the fighting. Meanwhile, statistics for the Japanese were far worse with two thirds of the 36,000 men in action in the region listed as dead or injured.

With Guadalcanal secure the Americans made for themselves a base from which to attack the main Japanese south Pacific headquarters at Rabaul. The direct threat posed by the enemy and its planes on Guadalcanal to Australia had been fended off.

And when he gets to Heaven
To St Peter he will tell:
'One more Marine reporting, Sir –
I've served my time in Hell.'
SGT JAMES A DONAHUE

CHAPTER THREE

New Guinea

The Kokoda track across the central massif of New Guinea presents one of the most daunting and diabolical terrains over which war was ever fought.

Kokoda

Map of New Guinea, with Kokoda arrowed. The name Kokoda would become synonymous with misery for Australian, US and Japanese troops.

The Battle of the Coral Sea ended one Japanese attempt to capture Port Moresby on New Guinea but did not end the empire's ambitions in the region. Japanese troops landed at Lae and Salamaua on New Guinea in March. Aware of the immediate threat, Australian commandos were promptly installed at Port Moresby and, by April 1942, two more Australian brigades were dispatched to join them while a further brigade was sent to Milne Bay, on the eastern tip of New Guinea. The challenge for those pouring into Port Moresby was to set off over the Owen Stanley Mountain range along the Kokoda track created by gold miners during the 1890s to reach Buna on the north west coast. The aim was to build an airstrip at Dobodura as a base for harassment of Japanese troop movements.

Before the Australians were even close to Buna, some 125 miles (200 km) across country from Port Moresby, the Japanese pre-empted the plan by landing there in droves in July. The setback at Midway meant it was more essential than ever before for the Japanese to seize New Guinea as far as their overall plans in the Pacific were concerned. A sizeable force forged up the Kokoda track from the north to meet the advancing Australians. Intelligence that indicated this was precisely the intention of the Japanese was casually disregarded by General Douglas MacArthur prior to the event. The same intelligence said that the Japanese believed they would be travelling by road through the Owen Stanley Mountains and the stark reality must have been a profound disappointment.

The Kokoda track presents one of the most daunting and diabolical terrains over which war was ever fought. It became a byword to express the deplorable depths of human misery. (Eventually, American

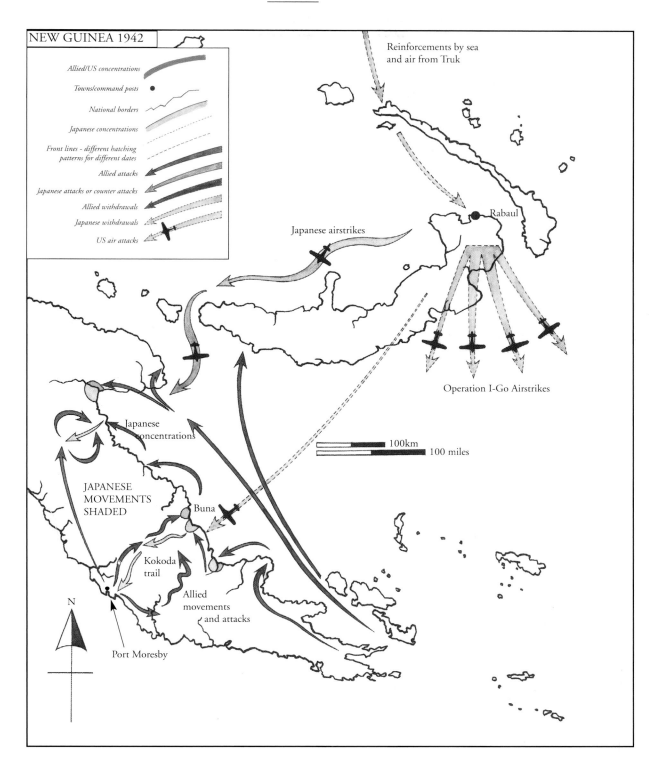

NEW GUINEA 1942

Allied/US concentrations
Towns/command posts
National borders
Japanese concentrations
Front lines - different hatching patterns for different dates
Allied attacks
Japanese attacks or counter attacks
Allied withdrawals
Japanese withdrawals
US air attacks

Reinforcements by sea and air from Truk

Rabaul

Japanese airstrikes

Operation I-Go Airstrikes

100km
100 miles

Japanese concentrations

JAPANESE MOVEMENTS SHADED

Buna

Kokoda trail

Allied movements and attacks

N

Port Moresby

influence in the area meant the track became better known as the trail.) Humidity, acutely steep landscapes, malarial swamps, leeches and incessant rain combined to create abhorrent conditions. Sometimes a gloom pervaded as the men went beneath a canopy of branches and vines. Where there were grasslands each blade cut like a razor. To add to their difficulties Australian servicemen had not been issued with jungle greens. Their khaki uniforms made them obvious targets in the foliage.

On 29 July the Japanese captured the

For the Emperor

Japanese troops dig in at Kokoda, 1942. Cut off from their supplies and reinforcements, the Japanese on New Guinea suffered appallingly.

immensely but the Japanese were perhaps worse off still. Supply lines were much longer for the Japanese than for the Australians, and American ships and submarines were devastating enemy shipping, with the consequence that Japanese soldiers were far more prone to disease and starvation. Hard fighting by the Australians prolonged the Kokoda track campaign beyond the expectations of the Japanese planners. Resources were also split between New Guinea and Guadalcanal, depriving both areas of badly needed equipment. In New Guinea the uniforms of Japanese fighters rotted to pieces on their bodies. There is even talk of cannibalism among the desperate Japanese forces fighting to stay alive in the hell of the Kokoda campaign.

By 25 August the startling pace of the Japanese was halted and it was their turn to withdraw. They were pursued by Australians whose fighting talents were judged to be lacking by the American commander MacArthur, who remained completely ignorant of the appalling conditions facing his men and the numerical superiority of the Japanese throughout. Curiously, he once reported to Washington that, among the Australians, 'aggressive leadership was lacking'. This from a man who did not step foot on New Guinea until October 1942. He was, of course, trying to save his own military career at the time.

Australians had no time to mark a tactical victory on the Kokoda track for at that precise moment some 2,000 Japanese marines were landed at Milne Bay, a different part of New Guinea, by way of a response to the US invasion of Guadalcanal. Their sights were set on the small but significant airfield there. The invasion force, to the astonishment of the

village of Kokoda, an approximate halfway point on the track with a small airstrip, and the Australians were propelled into a retreat. Now the action centred on Isurava, a village on the south side of Kokoda until that too was lost. Finally the Japanese pulled up before Imita Ridge, little more than 30 miles (50 km) short of Port Moresby.

The Australian contingent suffered

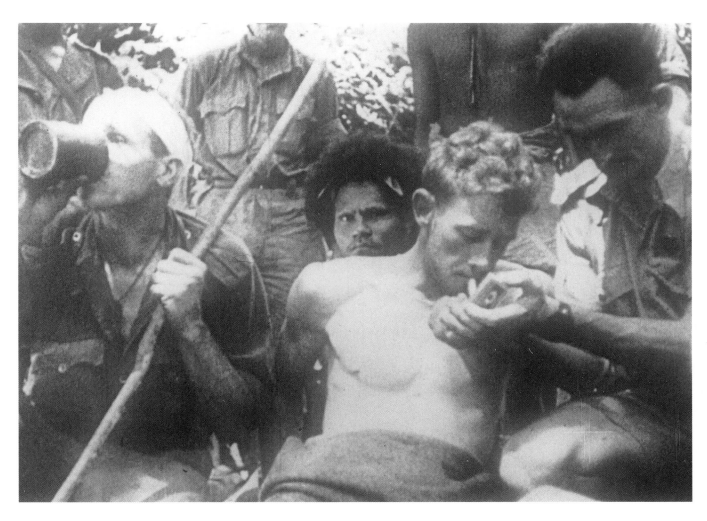

Australians there, included tanks and they broached the perimetre of the airfield. However, rain and mud bogged the heavy vehicles down and the redoubtable defenders finally drove the Japanese off. On 6 September the last Japanese survivors were evacuated. It was the first Japanese retreat of the conflict and it happened at the hands of the Australians backed by a small minority of US forces.

Back on the Kokoda trail the battle continued. The Australian cause was helped enormously by the local Melanesians who acted as barefoot porters, carrying equipment and even men with remarkable equanimity. A soldier's verse that appeared in an Australian newspaper gave the Papuan carriers and guides a new and affectionate name. 'May the mothers of Australia, When they offer up a prayer, Mention these impromptu angels, With their fuzzy wuzzy hair.' The fuzzy wuzzy angels were held in high regard by Australian soldiers who were dependent on them for survival.

Also on their side were Australian and American fighter planes capable of strafing the enemy on the narrow mountain paths. A constant bombardment of rain upon the earth made for some unstable conditions underfoot.

By now the mud at Namuro had been fashioned by Australian engineers into log-staked steps, each measuring between ten and 18 inches in height and dubbed the Golden Stairs. Nevertheless, even with the aid of the steps the gradients were breathtakingly steep. By 2 November the

On the Trail

Australian soldiers pause for a drink of water and a smoke amidst the 'green hell' of the Kokoda Trail.

Jungle Warfare

US troops move up to the front line at Buna, in the north of New Guinea.

Australians retook Kokoda from the Japanese. Now the tactical aim was to evict the Japanese from their remaining fortified strongholds at Buna, Gona and Sanananda. With the assistance of fresh Australian and American men, the battle for Buna was decided on 21 January 1943 after a desperately fought last ditch stand by the Japanese. The empire's ragged forces were once again in the business of evacuation, while for Australians and Americans it was all about successful consolidation. Although there were enemy footholds further east, the Japanese would not be returning to menace Port Moresby or Milne Bay.

The casualty list for the Japanese drive through New Guinea was an estimated 12,000 men, while some 5,700 casualties were recorded by the Australians and 2,800 by the Americans. While more Australians died in the Papua New Guinea offensive than in any other during the war, the Japanese were virutally eliminated. Yet for every battlefield casualty a further three men had fallen victim to tropical diseases or heat exhaustion. Had the Japanese succeeded in taking Milne Bay or conquering the Kokoda track then a blueprint to invade Australia may well have been resurrected by the Japanese high command. MacArthur was in no doubt that he was defending Australia from New Guinea. Now the Japanese were backing up the Pacific as the tidal currents changed direction.

Once again the role of the coast watchers had been pivotal.

As Eric Feldt explained:

'The success of the coast watchers was largely due to the experience of the personnel. Nearly all were men who had lived in the country, who knew it and the natives and who felt at home in it. It is easier to teach a man how to operate a teleradio or shoot a submachine gun than to teach him how to live in the jungle. The men, experienced and actually known to the natives, gained their help for it would be impossible to conduct such operations if the natives favoured the enemy. 'Throughout we had ready co-operation from other services. Aircraft dropped supplies to parties and sometimes picked them up; submarines and PT boats landed them and took them off, always with a steadiness and helpfulness which cannot be obtained by merely ordering an operation to be carried out. Without this co-operation, the coast watchers would have been gravely handicapped. 'Lastly there was help from the enemy. He was so stupid that he did not realise the damage that was being done to him and many times neglected to take measures against us and, by his own actions, alienated native sympathy. In fact, he was invaluable.'

Captured

Australian soldiers pose with captured Japanese flag after retaking the town of Wau on New Guinea, June 1943.

CHAPTER FOUR

Retreat and Reorganization

'In all the war I never received a more direct shock.'

WINSTON CHURCHILL ON THE SINKING OF THE BRITISH BATTLESHIP PRINCE OF WALES

In the wake of the attack at Pearl Harbor the Japanese rapidly began to make their presence felt at various locations around the South China Seas. Malaya, Burma, Singapore, Thailand, Hong Kong, the Philippines, the Dutch East Indies and Guam and Wake Islands were all on the shopping list drawn up by the Japanese military as prospective territories for the new, enlarged empire of the rising sun. There were a host of minor islands and atolls too, many of whose names have been swiftly forgotten by history, that fell under Japanese control, including Mereyon, Ponape Island and Mortlock. At this stage the Japanese would not countenance failure and were every bit as successful as they had anticipated.

Japanese aircraft were in action almost at once as the empire attempted to secure its advantage. Aware that US fighter planes based in the Philippines posed a threat to the plan, an attacking force was dispatched there on 8 December, catching numerous American aircraft parked up on the ground. In the short, sharp air offensive America lost more than half of their B-17 fleet and a further 86 other planes. Strategically it was perhaps as big a disaster as Pearl Harbor. Within the next 14 hours virtually all the areas earmarked for expansion by the Japanese were under fire.

An equivalent disaster soon pegged back the British plans for retaliation. Before Pearl Harbor a collection of ships known as 'Force Z' arrived in Singapore, partly in response to Churchill's concerns for the security of British provinces in the Far East. The pride of Force Z was the all-new battleship *Prince of Wales*, weighing in at an impressive 35,000 tons and capable of firing 60,000 shells a minute from its 175 anti-aircraft guns. It was accompanied by the battlecruiser *Repulse* and four destroyers. Significantly, there was an absence of aircraft carriers in the fleet, rendering the ships highly exposed to attack from enemy planes. The carrier proposed for the expedition had run aground in shallow waters at home and Churchill gambled that the high calibre of the *Prince of Wales* was sufficient to see off sea-borne opposition.

The first port of call for the mobilized Japanese land forces was Kota Bharu in northern Malaya, getting down to the serious business of invasion simultaneously with the attack on Pearl Harbor. On 8 December, Admiral Tom Spencer Vaughan Phillips decided to square up to the Japanese attackers at Kota Bharu, where the first Allied casualties of the war had already been claimed – the crew of a plane monitoring the Japanese fleet heading for Malaya were shot down by the Japanese.

If he could attack the enemy's ships while they were in the process of disgorging troops, Phillips believed, he could cause havoc. He reluctantly changed his plans in the belief that he had been spotted by Japanese planes, and set off for Singapore under cover of darkness. In fact, he hadn't been seen from the air, but his position had been noted by a prowling Japanese submarine attached to a Japanese fleet approaching from a different direction, but thanks to a co-ordinates error made by an unknown submariner, Japanese planes dispatched in search of the British ships failed to find them.

Phillip's luck did not hold out,

however. On 10 December he set off with another surprise attack in mind, this time at Kuantan on the Malay peninsula where he believed a Japanese attack was imminent. His information was bogus and he set a course for Singapore once more, maintaining such a strict radio silence to shield his position that even a request for air cover was not transmitted.

Another submarine spotted the British ships and this time their precise location was handed back to a Japanese aircraft carrier. At 11.20 am the first wave of Japanese bombers off-loaded on to the fleet. Damage was slight until the second wave of torpedo aircraft arrived twenty

Defence in Vain

British troops prepare for the defence of Singapore, December 1942. Due to bad intelligence and poor planning, however, this defence was almost wholly ineffective.

Loss of HMS *Prince of Wales* and HMS *Repulse*, 10 December 1941

Photograph taken from a Japanese aircraft during the initial high-level bombing attack. Repulse, *near the bottom of the view, has just been hit by one bomb and near-missed by several more.* Prince of Wales *is near the top of the image, generating a considerable amount of smoke.*

minutes later. The *Repulse* was the first craft to sink. She disappeared beneath the waves at 12.33 pm with the loss of 513 men. Less than an hour later *Prince of Wales*, a national treasure and something of a symbol of Britain's fortunes in the Far East, slipped to the bottom taking with her 327 men including Phillips. The destroyers picked up 1,285 survivors. Anti aircraft fire took down four attacking planes but victory belonged to the Japanese, primarily because the British ships had no aircraft with which to defend themselves. Afterwards Churchill admitted: 'In all the war I never received a more direct shock.' He had invested future hopes and plans with the ships that now,

at this critical moment, would come to nought. He would later say: 'There were no British or American capital ships in the Indian Ocean or the Pacific except the American survivors of Pearl Harbor who were hastening back to California. Over all this vast expanse of water Japan was supreme and we everywhere were weak and naked.'

The catastrophe coming at such an early stage in the war with Japan was keenly felt in Britain. It also provided an early indicator of Britain's shortcoming in the arena, namely, in the availability of aircraft. There were only 362 British aircraft in the Far East at the time. Those in Malaya, numbering 141, were utterly out-

Sinking Ship

Survivors of the Japanese attack on the battleship Prince of Wales *scramble for safety as the ship goes down beneath them, 10 December 1941.*

moded. Out of 22 airfields available to the British only seven were 'all weather' surfaces. The remaining 15 were grass and were frequently out of action following tropical downpours. Communications between the aircraft, bases and other armed services in the region were woefully lacking. Japanese progress through Malaya was phenomenally swift.

The action at Kota Bharu came slightly ahead of that in Pearl Harbor. It fell quickly to battle-hardened Japanese troops although British defenders put up considerable opposition, causing one Japanese colonel to call it 'one of the most violent actions of the Malaya Campaign.'

It was here the *Awagisan Maru*, a major transport ship, was sunk, the first Japanese vessel to come to grief in the embryonic conflict.

The Fall of Singapore and Hong Kong

Japanese movement through Malaya was indeed fast and fluid. On 11 January its capital Kuala Lumpur was abandoned to the enemy. By 31 January 1942 – less than two months after the offensive began – all the Commonwealth forces had been driven into Singapore where reinforcements were being made as quickly as conditions would allow. But the huge guns that defended the island were

The Fall of Singapore

British commander of the Singapore garrison, General Arthur Percival is escorted with his staff officers to sign the British surrender to the Japanese.

pointed out to sea. Defences on the landward side, where Japanese troops were threatening, were negligible.

By the time Britain surrendered Singapore, on 15 February 1942, its five 15 inch guns, 6 nine-inch guns and 14 six-inch guns still had not fired a shot.

Yet the defeat in Singapore came about not because of the way some guns were pointed but through the dispersal of the defenders on the island. There were some 85,000 in the British army and pitched against them just 30,000 Japanese troops. But the British had no tanks and inadequate aerial cover. Leading the Japanese was General Tomoyuki Yamashita, colloquially known as 'the Tiger' and believed by his men to be a military genius.

At the head of British troops was the ill-starred General Arthur Percival who was known among his troops as 'the rabbit'.

Churchill outlined his demands of the defenders: 'Not only must the defence of Singapore Island be maintained by every means but the whole island must be fought for until every single unit and every single strong point has been separately destroyed. Finally, the city of Singapore must be converted into a citadel and defended to the death. No surrender can be contemplated.'

He overlooked the obvious deficiencies in the defence of Singapore that should have been laid at the door of Whitehall. Anyway his words had little effect. On 8 February the Japanese began crossing the Johore Strait. Confused leadership had Allied defenders withdrawing from strong points and leaving a free path for the Japanese occupiers.

The Fall of Hong Kong

Mounted Japanese troops, led by Lieutenant General Sakai, enter Hong Kong on Christmas Day, 1941.

The British set alight the oil tanks in Singapore city to stop supplies falling into enemy hands. A black rain dropping from sinister dark clouds further depressed the spirits of the Allied fighters. When Percival received an air-dropped invitation to surrender it read: 'If you continue resistance it will be difficult to bear from a humanitarian point of view.' (It was all a bluff by Yamashita who feared that his troops would be overwhelmed unless the surrender came swiftly.)

This threat was sufficiently grim to persuade Percival to follow the Japanese rather than the Churchillian plan of action. The picture of him marching to greet the victorious Japanese with the Union flag held aloft alongside a white flag of surrender taunted a British public, who now had to face the harsh reality that Britain no longer had mastery of the seas, nor was she capable of protecting her colonies. Percival was cast into a political wilderness, something of a scapegoat for Britain's shortcomings.

The end of an Allied presence in Singapore effectively meant the end of ABDA, a first attempt at a combined Allied command representing American, British, Dutch and Australian interests, although it existed for a few more weeks. At its head had been Field Marshal Sir

Bataan Prisoners

US prisoners begin the infamous Bataan Death March, escorted by Japanese troops, April 1942.

Archibald Wavell, still out of favour with Churchill for what the British prime minister considered to be a poor performance in North Africa, but picked by Washington as the ideal man to be commander of a joint operation. Its failure was not a stain against Wavell. None of its members were prepared for battle.

Attention was momentarily focused away from this humiliation to another when, almost simultaneously with the fall of Singapore, two German battlecruisers – the *Scharnhorst* and the *Gneisenau* – along with the cruiser *Prinz Eugen* travelled in broad daylight up the English Channel through the Straits of Dover to their home ports at Wilhelmshaven in Germany. For the Allied troops who had surrendered on the island of Singapore, the ordeal was only just beginning.

About 80,000 Allied soldiers were taken prisoner, some of whom were so newly landed they had not fired a shot. One RAF man observed there were in any case no guns available for them to fight with. For them there were years ahead in the confines of a prisoner of war camp.

The attack against Hong Kong came on 8 December just six hours after Pearl Harbor. It was an obvious target, given the Japanese airbases handily placed at Formosa (Taiwan) from which to hit the colony. A request to MacArthur to make an early bombing raid on Formosa was turned down. The garrison of 4,400 Allied troops, including 800 Canadians, held fast until Christmas Day when they were finally overwhelmed by superior Japanese forces.

That same day Japanese forces landed in southern Thailand. Within 24 hours the Thai prime minister ordered his forces to end their resistance and within a month had declared war on Britain and America.

From Burma to the Philippines

Again on 8 December an initial attack against Wake Island was defended by resident US Marines. However, when the invaders returned on 23 December in substantial numbers the defenders were compelled to give up the fight.

Burma became a Japanese target on 14 December. The empire knew it would have India within its sights if it possessed Burma. By 8 March Rangoon was occupied and in June Akyab, important for its proximity to the Bay of Bengal and its airfields, fell to the Japanese.

The Borneo landings began on 15 December and the island fell to the Japanese two weeks later.

On 22 December the Japanese Fourteenth Army landed at Lingayen Gulf

At the Gates of Empire

Japanese troops assemble for the beginning of the invasion of Burma, December 1942– January 1943.

Le trombe dell'alba suonano l'inizio della marcia verso il confine orientale dell'India. Esso è stato varcato dalle truppe giapponesi il 10 gennaio. Lungo e il cammino che esse hanno già percorso dalla patria, e lungo è ancora quello che resta da percorrere in terra nemica, ma una volontà di ferro anima le mai stanche falangi dell'Imperatore.

Oilfields Burn

as the British destroy supplies to prevent them falling into Japanese hands during the retreat through Burma.

on Luzon, having previously taken control of numerous islands. Filipino troops of this newly independent nation were no match for the highly-trained Japanese. American troops based there withdrew from the capital Manila to mount a defence of the Bataan Peninsula. It was partially successful but bouts of malaria and poor morale left the Americans vulnerable. A Japanese offensive begun on 3 April secured the largest of the Philippine islands within six days.

Those Americans who were capable of escape, numbering in total some 15,000, withdrew further still to the island of Corregidor. The Japanese mounted artillery attacks and finally sent an invasion force to quell the opposition. By 9 June all resistance by the Americans and their Filipino allies had ended.

With so many Japanese bases around the region it became impossible for Allied ships to operate without being spotted and shot at. Japanese dominance was also helping Nazi Germany in its quest for raw materials to continue the war effort.

The New Year brought to Japan the acquisitions of Tarakan, Menado, Rabaul and Timor. Bali, Java and Sumatra were next in line. Where there were defenders, they were swiftly overwhelmed by superior manpower and fighting machines.

Into Burma

On 27 February came the Battle of the Java Sea, the first genuine naval engagement of the war and one of the few not fought entirely at night. It was not a distinguished display by the hastily assembled ABDA ships under the command of Rear Admiral Karel Doorman of the Netherlands. The Allied fleet was woefully short of air cover and could not match the Long Lance torpedoes possessed by the Japanese. Doorman perished during the initial clash when two cruisers and three destroyers were sunk. The following night the two remaining Allied cruisers, the Australian *Perth* and the *Houston* from America, sank two Japanese ships and damaged three others before being sunk themselves. The remaining ABDA ships were picked off by Japanese carrier aircraft and the invasion of the Dutch East Indies got underway.

With this initial flurry of activity out of the way the Japanese turned their attentions to Burma, held at the time as a colonial possession by Britain. There were numerous raw materials worth seizing in that country, including rubber, oil and tungsten, although it was not the battlefield of choice of the Japanese.

The attraction of Burma was two-fold. Decisive action would sever the Burma Road, an important supply route for the Chinese who were still part of a protracted war against Japan. That would ease the burden for the Japanese forces in China and possibly even open the way to an outright victory there, permitting more troops to enter the Pacific War.

Secondly there was the proximity of India, a wealthy subcontinent at the time in the hands of the British. The Japanese had good reason to imagine that nationalists would seize the opportunity to rise up against the colonial British, offering them access to new ports and troops. But it was undeniably difficult terrain for both attackers and defenders.

However, before long Rangoon had fallen to the Japanese and the Burma Road was in their hands. Ahead of them lay the longest retreat British forces had ever faced. In response Wavell invested the defensive hopes of the British empire into the Burma corps or Burcorps, comprising the 1st Burma Division and the 17th Indian Division. Happily there came the arrival of two experienced light tank regiments and an infantry battalion moved at speed from the Middle East to reinforce the Burcorps.

Without them the retreat would surely have been a rout. Burcorps, now under the command of Lieutenant General William Slim, followed the course of the Irrawaddy river back to the Indian border. With him went tens of thousands of Indian and Burmese refugees, harassed by some of the remaining Burmese population who were content to exchange one imperial master for another. The enemy forces were frequently no more than 24 hours behind. The monsoon season, that would wash away the roads and tracks vital for the retreat, was pending. The Allied troops adopted a scorched earth policy and destroyed everything rather than leave it to the Japanese. One estimate says that £11 million worth of oil and plant was destroyed in as little as 70 minutes. It was, of course, the oil that the Japanese were primarily interested in, forever in need of it to fuel their empire and all its outposts.

The overflying Japanese aircraft spread terror among those below. Japan was not only winning the combat but also the psychological war.

The Fall of Burma

Japanese troops on the attack at the oilfields of Yenangyaung, Burma, April 1942.

At the same time the Chinese armies were being driven back beyond Mandalay.

Not until after May 1942 could Burcorps properly regroup and return. They still suffered from scant resources and dented morale but the resolve at least among the high command was solid.

British problems were compounded by the presence of German U-boats in the Indian Ocean used both to pound British ships and to transport raw materials back to the Fatherland.

There was little good news to be had for the Allies in the winter of 1941 and the spring of 1942. Consequently, a hub-bub of domestic criticism was being heard about American lives being given fruit-

lessly for the benefit of other nations. President Roosevelt was unmoved by the objectors and engineered a robust defence of his war policies.

Marking the 210th anniversary of George Washington's birthday President Roosevelt broadcast to the nation, asking them to think big in terms of war effort:

'This war is a new kind of war. It is different from all other wars of the past, not only in its methods and weapons but also in its geography. It is warfare in terms of every continent, every island, every sea, every air-lane in the world . . .
'There are those who still think, however, in terms of the days of sailing ships.

They advise us to pull our warships and our planes and our merchant ships into our own home waters and concentrate solely on last ditch defense. But let me illustrate what would happen if we followed such foolish advice.

'Look at your map. Look at the vast area of China with its millions of fighting men. Look at the vast area of Russia with its powerful armies and proven military might. Look at the islands of Britain, Australia, New Zealand, the Dutch Indies, India, the Near East and the Continent of Africa, with their resources of raw materials. . . It is obvious what would happen if all of these great reservoirs of power were cut off from each other either by enemy action or by self-imposed isolation.'

The worse case scenario, as he outlined it, would be that China was left to struggle without aid against Japan, and Australia, New Zealand and the Dutch East Indies would quickly fall under Japanese domination, permitting the empire to devote its resources to other plans of attack:

'Those Americans who believed that we could live under the illusion of isolationism wanted the American eagle to imitate the tactics of the ostrich. Now, many of those same people, afraid that we may be sticking our necks out, want our national bird to be turned into a turtle. But we prefer to retain the eagle as it is — flying high and striking hard.'

Generals Confer

General Sir Archibald Wavell (right), Commander in Chief for India, meeting with General Sir Claude Auchinleck, Commander in Chief for the Middle East, to discuss the war situation, January 1942.

CHAPTER FIVE

The Arakan Campaign

The fighting in the so-called Admin Box in the Arakan region was the first major British victory against the Japanese and helped to destroy the myth of the Japanese superman.

They Shall Not Pass

Sikh troops of 7th Indian Division defend the Ngakyeduak Pass following the Japanese offensive of 6 February 1944.

In the closing months of 1942 the British decided upon a thrust back into Burma. The result in a nutshell was that the British and Indian troops were outfought, outmanoeuvred and pushed back. More than 900 soldiers were killed and a further 4,000 were wounded in the ill-starred campaign. At the same time Japanese casualty figures were much lower standing at 1,100 with 400 dead or missing. A Japanese thrust into the malarial territories of Arakan in March 1943 was repulsed, but once again British losses were twice as high as the Japanese.

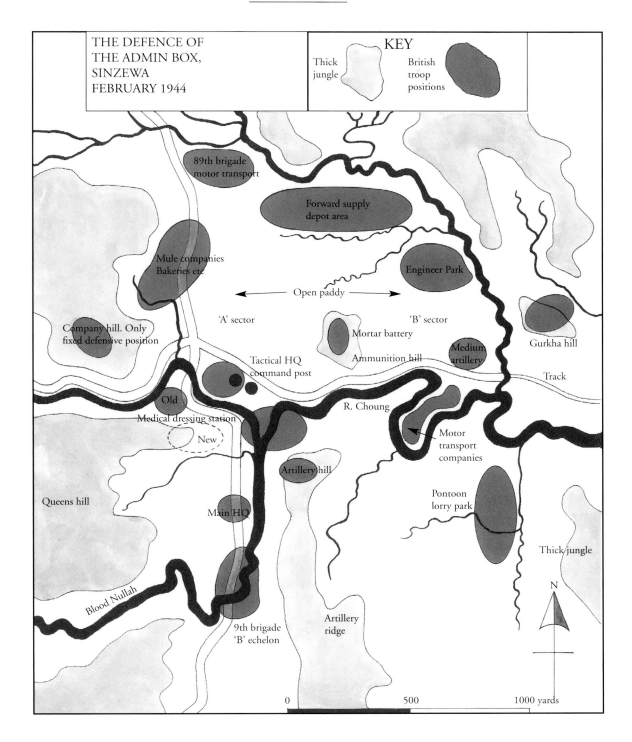

THE DEFENCE OF
THE ADMIN BOX,
SINZEWA
FEBRUARY 1944

KEY

Thick jungle

British troop positions

89th brigade motor transport

Forward supply depot area

Mule companies Bakeries etc

Engineer Park

Open paddy

'A' sector

'B' sector

Gurkha hill

Company hill. Only fixed defensive position

Mortar battery

Medium artillery

Tactical HQ command post

Ammunition hill

Track

Old

R. Choung

Medical dressing station

New

Motor transport companies

Artillery hill

Queens hill

Pontoon lorry park

Main HQ

Thick jungle

Blood Nullah

N

9th brigade 'B' echelon

Artillery ridge

0   500   1000 yards

Many of the British troops believed the jungle was as much of an enemy to them as the Japanese. The sounds and smells among the steamy vegetation were alien and frightening. While the Japanese soldiers were entirely comfortable eating bamboo shoots which sprouted in abundance in the jungle, the British Tommy anticipated meat, vegetables and, where possible, Yorkshire puddings. Meat like corned beef was supplied to the soldiers. But when they opened a tin of it the contents frequently poured out in liquid form having melted in the heat and the troops remained hungry. They were also unaccustomed to other jungle foods and fruits

Surprise Attack

15th Indian Division mount a surprise attack on Japanese positions, by landing eight miles up the Ma-Chiang river near Latpan.

while the Japanese were more likely to take advantage of them.

To the British eye, the Japanese appeared to have no fear of guns or death. With rations that amounted to hardly more than a handful of rice they seemed to flourish rather than diminish as the struggling Allied troops did. They obeyed orders without question and were willing to fight on when all hope had gone. For a while it seemed that the Japanese were a breed of indestructible supermen who were sure to come out on top.

It was this underlying conviction that British officers had to countermand. The charismatic General William Slim, richly experienced and now in command of the newly-formed Fourteenth Army did much to rejuvenate his men.

He was part of the South East Asia Command structure defined at the end of 1943 and led by Admiral Lord Louis Mountbatten. Although he had some evident shortcomings, Mountbatten was very engaged with the troops and seemed able to lift their flagging spirits.

Other factors were now also weighing in on the side of the British. Significantly, the capacity to ship supplies via the North East India Railways network had by now increased about eight fold, easing the military's logistical problems in the region.

More crucially still, the RAF had taken delivery of new aircraft including Spitfires and Hurricanes, which would lend its pilots mastery of the Asian skies. The aerial dinosaurs that so singularly let down the defenders of Malaya and Singapore were at last committed to history. Alongside American fliers the RAF enjoyed a dominance that had hitherto been lacking.

In February 1944 the British had once again ventured into Burma, optimistically citing the airfields at Akyab as their target, to use as a base for an eventual thrust to retake Rangoon. Their secondary objective was to clear the Maugdaw Peninsula of Japanese forces.

At the same time the Japanese began a move of their own into Arakan, primarily as a diversion for a planned attack on India. They happened across the administration and supply base set up by the 7th Indian Division at Sinzweya to assist the forward troops heading for Akyab and launched a surprise attack.

In common with most administrative bases, it was some distance behind the British lines. The element of shock and awe among the British was immense. Once again the Japanese proved themselves masters of camouflage and concealment. Vigilant aerial reconaissance by the British could do nothing to pinpoint the stealthy Japanese. Before long the Ngakyedauk Pass that linked the 7th Indian Division to other elements in the army was in Japanese hands. Soon the British were encircled and there was bitter fighting around what became known as the 'Admin Box'. Within it the Allied soldiers locked in fearful combat were for the most part clerks, mechanics, drivers and even a general.

Wavell gave orders that this withdrawal would be limited to 'boxes', which were to be defended. Slim's Japanese counterpart was even more strident on the subject, as an order given by him that month and intercepted by the British reveals:

'Whatever situation you are in you fight to the last. Keep on firing till your last round has gone. Then fight with your sword. When your sword is broken turn yourself into a human bullet and charge into the enemy. Keep shouting "Long live the Emperor" until the very end. Then you can die bravely.'

A new tactic was employed by the Allies, that of supplying soldiers in remote areas from the air. Cargo was parachuted in, usually with commendable accuracy and that averted certain defeat. Eventually the forces in the box were joined by tanks as British and Indian forces pressed down to assist, ultimately threatening to encircle the Japanese.

The aerial drops were, as Churchill put it, like manna from heaven. Indeed, they were both physical and psychological lifelines to the soldiers isolated by enemy action in unforgiving terrain. During the battle of the Admin Box some 2,000 tons of food, fuel and ammunition were dispatched to the defenders. In the same period more than 5,000 casualties were evacuated to India, all for the loss of a single Dakota. For their part the Japanese began well but took with them just ten days supplies, no tanks and no artillery. The option of aerial drops was also not available, given the Allied superiority in the air. The net result was that no British withdrawal was forced and the 7th Division stayed put. Ultimately the Japanese themselves had to pull back, travelling in small groups to evade detection. They left 5,000 dead behind. Britain had won its first military triumph over the Japanese.

Churchill seized on the victory, sending the following congratulatory telegram to Admiral Lord Louis Mountbatten, appointed supreme commander of the newly created South East Asia Command in October 1943:

I sent you today my public congratulations on the Arakan fighting. I am so glad this measure of success has attended it. It is a sign of the new spirit in your forces and will, I trust, urge everyone to keep closer to the enemy . . .

At Arakan there came the first Japanese surrenders, a sight Allied soldiers believed they would never see. Still, those who waved the white flag were still in the minority. The notion of surrender – no matter how eminently sensible it was as a life-preserving course of action – was a matter for shame by Japanese standards. Each Japanese serviceman had pledged his life to the emperor and to give up the fight would mean dishonouring the empire's divine ruler. Doctors tending wounded Japanese soldiers learned they had to bind their patients' hands or bandages would be ripped off in a suicide bid. As they healed the reluctant prisoners sought new ways of achieving death with honour, usually involving a hand grenade or the like. Of course, their bid to serve the emperor often posed a threat to their captors who were doing everything to keep them alive.

Prisoners of the Japanese

Meanwhile Allied soldiers who surrendered to the Japanese were, quite simply, despised by their captors, and often treated appallingly, as has been well-documented. Some captured Sikh troops fought for Japan rather than be thrown into one of the notorious prison camps.

Others refused and joined the vast number who were dispatched to build the Burma railway. Even today the name conjures up images of grime and grind, with prisoners working up to 18 hours a day to fulfill the Japanese dream of a track between Thanbyuzayat in Burma to Nong Pladuk in Thailand to form an additional much-needed supply route. The track had to be cut through 260 miles (420 km) of mountainous jungle in torrid conditions.

The punishments meted out for slacking or insubordination were harsh. Some of the beatings administered viciously to men weakened by lack of proper food and sanitation were fatal.

Many of the men suffered from ulcers that stubbornly refused to heal. Their sole option was to drop maggots – in plentiful supply – into the wounds until the oozing pus had been eaten away. This was by no means the worst of ailments. Dysentery, malaria, cholera and dehydration all prevailed in one season or another. Those who escaped illness or recovered from it were still hit hard by the effects of poor nutrition. As time went on once robust bodies turned to skin-covered skeletons. Sometimes the spirit was utterly broken by this appalling existence. One man recalls a fellow soldier who chose to commit suicide by putting his head down a well-soiled latrine and drowning. Later, captive medic Lieutenant Colonel Edward 'Weary' Dunlop gave a personal view of the Australians he knew in the prison camps:

I can say that the Australians outworked and outsuffered any nationality on that accursed river (Kwai). I hardly ever saw a man refuse to go out in another's place or a man's spirit break until the time came to turn his face to the wall.

In fact, his assessment may be awry. For while Allied prisoners suffered immense deprivation the Asian labourers brought in from other corners of the empire by the conquerors faced even more stringent demands. Some 70,000 died during the building of the Burma railway, alongside an estimated 12,000 British, Australian, American and Dutch detainees. The line was completed in October 1943, bombed by Allied aircraft in 1944 and abandoned in early 1945.

It has since been said that every sleeper laid cost a human life. Allied prisoners were left wondering why the treatment was so sadistic when they would have built the railway just as well or perhaps even faster in decent conditions.

The railway in Burma is the most famous example of (illegal) forced labour but does not stand alone. Hugh Trebble, a Royal Air Force clerk taken prison in Java, was sent to build a track across Sumatra:

We had to work 16 hours a day, seven days a week. We had a bowl of rice in the morning and a bowl of rice at night and it was all we had to live on. At our base camp we used to bury about 16 men a day.
When we were building the railway we were beaten with rails and spanners. The thing to do was to stay conscious. If you fell over and blacked out you were beaten and could get badly injured. One of the guards was so short he would make you stand in a monsoon drain in order to beat you.

It was a matter of some pride to Trebble and his fellow prisoners that they managed to wreck no fewer than three full sized steam locomotives in outrageously staged accidents as they worked.

Numerous prisoners were transported to the Japanese home islands, including British captain M. P. Murphy captured at Singapore. Excerpts from his diaries highlight the horrors of the journey made in

August 1942 in the hold of a ship.

My legs are badly swollen right up to the hips with beri beri and am in poor shape after the fever, probably eight and a half stones at most. We were issued with warm suits and what trash! Appears to be made from straw gossamer and pulls apart. No use to anyone. We embarked about 12 into hell again, to join a party of about 200 Americans from the Philippines, the survivors of Bataan and Corregidor – and what a mess of humanity. Shocking, we are bad but they seem much worse and have lost all control from starvation and ill treatment . . .
Impossible to describe the foulness. Drinking water rationed and no washing water… Seems impossible that we can survive this awful filth for long. Food, dysentery, fever, no means of keeping anything clean. Latrine accommodation only three cubicles for 2,500 and with the dysentery and diarrhoea…

About 20 died on the six day journey. Conditions were better but far from ideal in the camp. There were 500 men to one bath, no fires, a diet of rice and cabbage and few cigarettes. The highlight of the year was the arrival of the Red Cross parcels on Christmas Eve. Murphy describes the contents of one:

What joy when the parcels were given out this evening. Sixteen items but no smokes, – lb chocolate, 2oz cheese, 3oz chicken and ham paste, 1lb jam pudding, 1lb boiled beef, 8 oz Peak Frean biscuits, lb turtle galantine, lb margarine, 12 oz tin milk, 8oz bacon, 12 oz apple and plum jam, 12 oz tin tomatoes, 2oz Maypole tea, 4oz Tate sugar, one bar soap, one pkt barley sugar. Another death but no one seems to take any notice of deaths now.

CHAPTER SIX

The Chindits

'Throughout the history of war the number of leaders who have invented a new technique of warfare is small indeed: Wingate, with his Long Distance Penetration groups, will rank as one of them.'

ORDE WINGATE OBITUARY, DAILY TELEGRAPH, 1 APRIL 1944

Chindits

Brigadier Orde Wingate briefing men of 77th Indian Brigade at an airfield at Sylhet in Assam before an operation. With him is Colonel Philip Cochrane USAAF, responsible for the air transport for the brigade's operations.

Orthodox military thinking had left Britain on the back foot in Burma. Something a little out of the ordinary was needed, militarily speaking, to pep up a sagging campaign. It came in the form of the Chindits, ordinary soldiers who fought in extraordinary situations, and their commander Orde Wingate.

Experienced in guerilla warfare and acquainted with the Burmese terrain, Wingate was prepared to take the Japanese on at their own game of infiltration and surprise attack. His aim was to gear up the ponderously-titled Long Range Penetration Group to see what havoc might be created by relatively small groups of men capable of effective ambush and swift retreat. His succinct credo was that the Chindits should be 'a hand in the enemy's bowels'.

Wingate himself came up with the distinctive name, derived from the word for the winged creatures said to guard Burmese pagodas, chinthe.

Now it was applied to the 77th Infantry Brigade, comprising the 13th King's (Liverpool) Regiment, 3/2nd Ghurka Rifles, 142 Commando Company, 2nd Burma Rifles, eight RAF sections, a Brigade signal section from the Royal Corps of Signals and a mule transport company who embarked on the First Chindit Expedition. (These men tended to call themselves 'Wingate's Follies' or sometimes 'Wingate's Raiders'.) Codenamed Operation *Longcloth*, the expedition departed from Imphal in India on 8 February 1943.

Wingate sent his men into Burma with the tasks of cutting the railway line between Mandalay and Myitkyina, crossing the Irrawaddy river to cut the rail link between Mandalay and Lashio and also harassing the enemy in the Shwebo area. They left with his rousing phrases ringing in their ears:

It is always a minority that occupies the front line. It is a still smaller minority that accepts with a good heart tasks like this that we have chosen to carry out. We need not, therefore, as we go forward into conflict suspect ourselves of selfish or interested motives. We have all had the opportunity of withdrawing and we are here because we have chosen to be here; that is, we have chosen to bear the burden and heat of the day. Men who make this choice are above the average in courage. We need therefore have no fear for the staunchness and guts of our comrades.
Our motive may be taken to be the desire to serve our day and generation in the way that seems nearest to our hand. The battle is not always to the strong nor the race to the swift.

Victory in war cannot be counted upon but what can be counted upon is that we shall go forward determined to do what we can to bring this war to the end which we believe best for our friends and comrades in arms, without boastfulness or forgetting our duty, resolved to do the right so far as we can see the right.

The men were divided between the Northern Group 2,000 strong with 850 mules and the Southern group of 1,000 men and 250 mules. Then there were further divisions into columns, each comprising some 400 men, a platoon of Burma Rifles to provide reconnaissance, two mortars and two Vickers machine guns, some 120 mules, an RAF liaison officer and radio operators to summon air supplies, a doctor and a further radio detachment.

Taking into account the extremely challenging circumstances in which they were made, the Allied air drops, made in clearings and on occasion in the jungle itself, achieved considerable success in keeping the troops behind enemy lines supplied, and virtually no aircraft were lost during this phase of *Longcloth*. The rations for the men on the ground remained in short supply, however, and conditions across the board remained extremely harsh.

As planned, the Japanese were surprised by the incursions made by Chindits. Initially they believed the men to be militarily unimportant, just small commando groups sent to gather intelligence and to act as an irritant. But as damage to railway bridges and outposts continued to mount the Japanese realized something bigger was afoot. The aim was then to isolate the British troops by cutting the supply lines out of India.

Behind Enemy Lines

A Chindit column crossing a Burmese river, deep in enemy territory, 1943. Through their tactical successes behind enemy lines, the Chindits showed that the much-feared Japanese army could be taken on and defeated.

Of course, the Japanese presumed these were overland and committed a number of men to this fool's errand. Only when an airdrop was witnessed by chance by some Japanese soldiers could a full complement of men devote themselves to rooting out the Chindits.

On 24 March Wingate was ordered to withdraw, not least because their progress had left a number of the columns at the very edge of aircover. Dumping equipment and turning loose mules, the Chindits tried to lighten their loads. However, many of the men were now weak through illness, exhaustion or poor nutrition. The journey home, back over the Rivers Chindwin and Irrawaddy, remained treacherous.

Out of 3,000 officers and men that set out from Imphal four months previously just 2,182 returned in May and June, each having walked between 1,000 and 1,500 miles. Only about a quarter remained fighting fit.

By his own high standards, Wingate judged the mission to be a failure, primarily for the loss of good fighting men. The propaganda value of the first Chindit expedition was, however, immense. It was the first time the Allies had employed guerrilla-style tactics and they had found some measured success. It was also the first fight back orchestrated by the Allies against the thus-far invulnerable Japanese. Morale among the British began creeping up. Although it wasn't clear at the time, Japan's Lieutenant General Renya Mutaguchi felt sufficiently pressured by the First Chindit Expedition to rush an attack into India before his army was sufficiently prepared so that it was always doomed to failure.

Luminaries including Churchill judged the episode so successful that there was all-round agreement among the dignitaries of the Quebec conference in 1943, which the prime minister attended with Wingate, that another should take place. Lessons had to be learned from the first expedition, like the need for a better evacuation plan for the wounded. Many injured men were left behind in Burma to be tended by local people. This, of course, put the wounded and the carers in jeopardy. (One of the greatest fears of the men under Wingate's control was the prospect of being wounded and abandoned.) A pledge for greater air support was forthcoming, much to Wingate's satisfaction.

A second expedition was organized, scheduled to return to north Burma in March 1944. This time more troops were involved – the equivalent of six brigades rather than one as per the first outing. Each brigade was made up from various regiments and alongside the Lancashire Fusiliers and the King's Own Royal stood the Gurkha Rifles and the Cameroonians.

According to the *Daily Mail* newspaper of 21 May 1943 the Chindits had:

...penetrated to within 60 miles of Mandalay, blown up the Mandalay-Myitkyina railway in 75 places, destroyed four railway bridges, and blocked the famous Bongyaung Gorge [and]...killed at least 200 Japanese. Meanwhile, they kept a whole Japanese division of 15,000 men occupied in hunting for them to prevent their reaching the Lashio railway.

Air Drop

Dropping supplies to Chindit units, deep behind the Japanese lines. Air drops such as this played a crucial role in the successes of Wingate's men.

Once again aerial drops were going to be key to survival. However, air traffic could only move when the weather conditions were right. Tropical conditions, especially the monsoon season, worked against this telling strategy. If planes were grounded the Chindit operation suffered setbacks, although fortunately these proved redeemable.

Churchill described to Roosevelt in a letter the launch of the second Chindit campaign, and how two Long Range Penetration brigades dropped into the jungle 100 miles inside enemy territory:

The first landings were made by gliders, whose occupants then prepared the strips to receive transport aircraft. Between 6 March and 11 March seven thousand five hundred men, with all their gear and with mules, were successfully landed. The only losses were a number of the gliders and some of these should be reparable. The brigades have now started their advance but a small holding party has been left at one of the strips to receive a flight of Spitfires and a squadron of Hurricanes which were to fly in to protect the base and provide air support.

The only serious mishap occurred on the first night. One of the strips in the northern area was found to have been obstructed by the Japanese, and the surface of the remaining strip was much worse than was expected, causing crashes which blocked the strip and prevented further landings that night. A few of the gliders had to be turned back in the air and failed to reach out territory. Another strip was immediately prepared in this area and was ready for landing two days later. The total of killed, wounded and missing is at most 145.

Once again each column would have about 400 men with some weaponry, a reconnaissance platoon and signaller and medical detachments.

One of the primary aims was to disrupt supplies and thus prevent a wholesale Japanese advance into India. Chindit action would also assist the troops at Ledo pushing forward into northern Burma at American instigation with road builders advancing in their wake to create an important new supply route and oil pipe line. Their presence would also be an asset to Chinese troops pressing the Japanese from the north-east.

Just weeks into the second campaign the charismatic Wingate was killed in an air crash aged 41. He was one of nine men who died when a US transport plane crashed in India on 25 March.

In a report carried by the *Daily Mail* at the time his wife spoke about her husband and his military ethos:

People say to me that my husband was unorthodox but this isn't strictly correct. He is rather orthodox in an unusual way.
He has been described as another Lawrence of Arabia but again I don't agree. I rather think he is more like Cromwell. He has always maintained that contact between a commander and his men is absolutely neces-sary to the success of any venture. Cromwell's motto: 'Know what you fight for and love what you know' has been his throughout his life…
He has been a soldier for more than 20 years. During the last 10 years he did little else but perfect his ideas of using highly trained and superbly equipped forces in an irregular way.'

Wingate fought in Sudan, Palestine and Ethiopia before being dispatched to Burma by Wavell. Having been injured in Ethiopia and enduring the effects of malaria he had attempted to take his own life, but recovered to fulfil Wavell's great hopes. General Sir William Slim, who knew him in Africa and Asia, described him as 'strange, excitable, moody creature but he had a fire in him. He could ignite other men.'

Former Chindit Bob Cartwright remembers: 'Everyone thought the world of Orde Wingate, the man behind the Chindits, even though he wasn't liked by the big shots in India. All they did was criticize him.'

His rocky relationship with other members of the army top brass led to

A Way Through

Bombed entrance to a tunnel where British and Indian troops captured a major highway.

Digging In

Chindit unit with Vickers machine gun behind enemy lines, dug in by a railway track and awaiting the Japanese army.

speculation that the aircraft he travelled in had been sabotaged although no evidence ever came forward to support this. His remains and those of the rest killed that day were at first buried in Imphal. In 1950 the bodies were taken to Washington for re-interment at Arlington National Cemetery.

On 1 April 1944 the *Daily Telegraph* also carried news of his death, observing:

'At this juncture, when his methods are under trial for the first time on a large scale, his death is a particularly tragic loss, which the Allied cause can ill afford to bear. Throughout the history of war the number of leaders who have invented a new technique of warfare is small indeed: Wingate, with his Long Distance Penetration groups, will rank as one of them.'

In fact, these techniques that Wingate pioneered were serving British forces well

and were causing some considerable confusion in the ranks of the Japanese. There was, however, always the threat of a counter attack.

On 13 May 1944, 47 Column, comprising of men from the Leicester Regiment, were ambushed in their bivouac by a patrol from the Japanese 53rd Division. At its end two officers, a sergeant major and six privates were killed. A further 13 men were wounded, including Harold Lambert who had been shot in the lower leg.

Much later he described the incident:

There was a hell of a racket, some were still asleep, others were brewing up when all hell let loose. At first I didn't realize how badly I'd been wounded. I was more concerned for the mule that was carrying all the column's money – it was so badly wounded it had to be shot. A major tried to lead a counter attack but as he stood up he fell dead with a bullet through the head. We then dispersed further into the jungle. I was lucky as I could still walk after a fashion. Lots of Japanese were killed and as we scrambled up a steep mountainside and over a river we lost lots of mules, either through falls or drowning.

The column swiftly regrouped and soon made contact with another column further west. With the skill of his own column's Medical Officer and the help of those in the next column, who were from Nigerian brigades, he managed to survive the ordeal. Eventually he was evacuated by light aircraft from an airstrip on the shores of Lake Inawgyi, helping to prove that flaws with getting the wounded to safety revealed by the first expedition had been remedied by the second.

Rodney Tatchell, of the Royal Engineers, was also a Chindit and remembered the experience in blunt terms:

Life in the Chindits was extremely simple. To prepare oneself for bed one simply spread a groundsheet, took off one's boots, made a pillow of one's pack and one's inflated 'Mae West' and rolled oneself in one's blanket. Getting up was just the reverse procedure. It was often anything up to three weeks before one had the chance of an all-over wash in a stream. From December 1943 to May 1944 I never slept on anything but the ground with just the sky above – if you could see it through the roof of the jungle.

In his opinion, the key to Chindit survival was the air support now lent by the Americans:

It is impossible to exaggerate the value to us of this private air force. We depended on the US Dakotas in conjunction with the RAF for our vital supply drops, on the light planes for evacuating our casualties and on the Mustang close support aircraft for tackling anything beyond our own resources. We were ourselves lightly armed, our biggest weapons being medium machine guns and three-inch mortars. If we struck a strongly-defended enemy post which needed something more powerful . . . all we had to do was to call up air base for dive-bombers, mark the target with a mortar smoke bombs and the Mustangs would soon arrive and blast hell out of the opposition.

The Chindits were now led by Joe Lentaigne, a fine commander but not a Wingate. Nor would he commit the men to highly ambitious plans behind enemy lines in the way Wingate would have. Faced with exhausted men and an effective Japanese attack at Indaw, three brigades were amalgamated into one to counter the emerging threat. Then the matter of premature withdrawal was investigated and agreed.

Even then, the Chindits had once again been a costly nuisance to the Japanese. Afterwards, Japanese military experts praised the timing of the Second Expedition. Had it occurred just a few days earlier troops earmarked for the forthcoming attack on Imphal would most likely have been kept back to deal with the roaming Chindits. As it was, they were now too distant to be of practical assistance. A week later and the essential equipment for troops at Imphal would have escaped the attentions of the Chindits and passed unimpeded through to Imphal, possibly weighting the balance in Japan's favour.

CHAPTER SEVEN

The Gilbert and Marshall Islands

The invasion of the Marshall Islands would be the first time the Americans had assaulted Japanese soil; they knew the fanaticism with which the Japanese would fight.

President Roosevelt had initially held off from the prospect of an invasion of the territories occupied by the Japanese. Earlier in the war he had taken note of British opposition to an immediate attack on occupied Europe and the joint focus of the war at that stage became North Africa. To the dismay of some he told his advisors: 'If we can't invade northern Europe we must go somewhere else and that somewhere else is not the Pacific.'

He was understandably cautious about the immense distances involved in the Pacific, the necessity for a rock solid supply chain and adequate aerial cover, a perpetual shortage of landing craft, the vulnerability of amphibious operations to a strong navy, and much else besides.

But by the spring of 1943 that stated policy was outdated. Japanese naval power had been largely disabled while the army's efforts were now regularly being blunted. In March 1943 the Battle of the Bismarck Sea had done much to assist. A convoy on its way from Rabaul to New Guinea was attacked from the air by a variety of Allied air craft that annihilated four destroyers and eight transports. The remaining men were forced back to their home base and the air superiority of the Allies was amply illustrated.

After Guadalcanal was secured American forces looked further up the island chain to Bougainville and New Britain. It was all part of Operation *Cartwheel* to mop up Japanese resistance in that section of the Pacific and to eliminate Rabaul, the most important Japanese base in the region. It was a two-pronged assault with General MacArthur clearing the Huon peninsular in New Guinea and Admiral Halsey steering through the Solomons. By the time the Americans were in a position to invade, Rabaul had been virtually evacuated. The Americans bypassed the port and moved on. The war in the South Pacific was over.

The Aleutian Islands

The Aleutian Islands of Attu and Kiska lying south of Alaska had been occupied by the Japanese since June 1942. Significantly both were US territory and the urge to recapture them was great. On 11 May the 7th US Infantry Division landed on Attu amid aerial bombardments from aircraft carrier planes. Japanese resistance was dogged although before the end of the month the troops had been pushed on to the highest ground. In the face of large numbers of enemy troops and the certainty of defeat

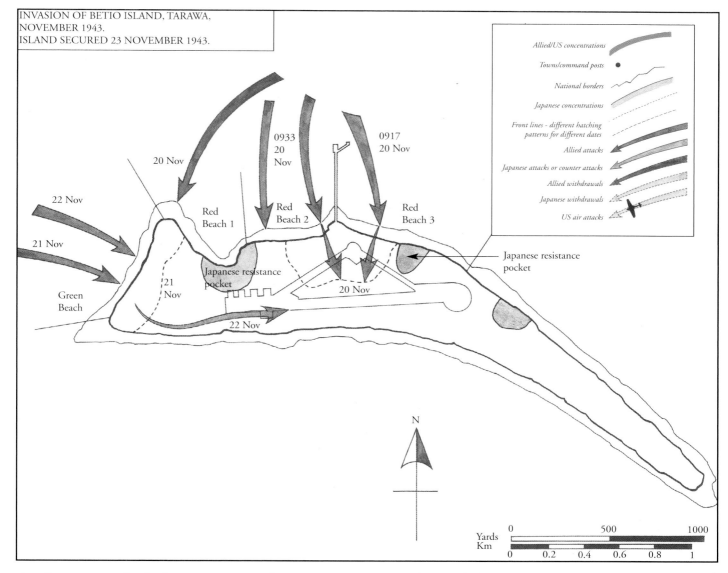

INVASION OF BETIO ISLAND, TARAWA, NOVEMBER 1943.
ISLAND SECURED 23 NOVEMBER 1943.

the Japanese embarked on a series of banzai charges on 29 May, literally suicidal dashes at the Americans in pursuit of an honourable death. In doing so they overran two command posts and a medical station before being brought down. Another day-long battle saw the island secured. Just 28 prisoners were taken by the Americans and a total of 2,351 Japanese bodies were found. American casualties amounted to 600 dead and 1,200 wounded.

With some trepidation the US forces under Vice Admiral Thomas Kincaid set about trying to secure Kiska, initially with a sea blockade and aerial bombardments.

However, on 28 July – while US navy patrols were refuelling – the Japanese defenders numbering some 5,183 soldiers and civilians were evacuated to safety under a blanket of fog. Air reconnaissance failed to detect an absence of enemy troops so an amphibious assault was mounted on 15 August involving 34,000 US and Canadian troops. More than 50 were killed in friendly fire incidents before it was established the island was vacant. On the positive side, it was another exercise in amphibious assaults, which were even now providing valuable lessons to the Americans that would help to save lives later on.

Operation *Galvanic*

Now the target for the Allies was the Gilbert and Marshall Islands, disparate islets and atolls scattered more centrally in the Pacific between the Solomons and Hawaii. First in line was the Gilbert Islands, a British colony until the arrival of the Japanese.

Operation *Galvanic* with the twin objectives of Makin and Tarawa began on 20 November 1943, following a comprehensive bombardment from both aircraft and battleships. These signalled the begin-

ning of one of the war's epic battles, the human cost of which stunned the world.

At Makin a 6,472 invasion force commanded by three majors surnamed Smith got the better of 848 defenders in four days. The swift success secured with few land-based casualties enabled Army General R. C. Smith to radio the navy task force 'Makin taken'.

At sea the Japanese claimed the escort carrier *Liscome Bay*, which was sunk with the loss of 644 lives, and the light carrier *Independence* which had to retire for repair.

Coming Ashore

US Marines of the 2nd Division come ashore at Tarawa, on the island of Betio. The Japanese garrison was well-entrenched in the rock of the island, and would resist to the last man.

Advance with Caution

US Marines move cautiously into the interior of Betio Island, ever aware of the presence of Japanese snipers.

But 100 miles to the south it was a different story unfolding at the same time. The grim statistics of the battle were all the more galling, given the size of Tarawa. The key garrison of Tarawa was on the main island of Betio, something similar in size to New York's Central Park. But on it 4,500 elite Japanese troops had dug themselves in to an intricately designed and cunningly disguised bunker system and they proved difficult to dislodge. Indeed, the defences were so staunch that one Japanese commander, Rear-Admiral Shibasaki Keiji believed that one million men thrown at it during one hundred years still would not triumph.

He was wrong, of course, but his view underlined the determination with which the Japanese would defend their strongholds. The small area was indeed saturated by bombs and incendiaries but its fortified positions remained largely unscathed.

Technical glitches meant the Marines were unable to direct the naval fire where it counted.

Men of the 2nd Marine Division were also grievously hampered by an incorrect prediction in the height of the tides. Men forced to wade ashore when their landing craft got hooked on to coral reefs died in droves under the weight of Japanese gunfire. LVTs were used as armoured personnel carriers for the first time and this was a successful tactic. But there were too few of them to make a real difference.

For a while it looked like the American forces would be tossed back into the sea. However, a communications breakdown prevented a full-on Japanese counter attack on the first night. In turn that allowed the Marines to establish positions on the shore.

Land based Marines then protected the arrival of reinforcements that ultimately

Captured

A rare image of Japanese prisoners, taken on Betio Island. Most Japanese soldiers considered death infinitely preferable to the dishonour of surrender.

overwhelmed the Japanese, whose last hope once again lay in banzai charges.

By 23 November the island was conquered, at the cost of a US casualty list numbering 1,009 dead and 2,101 wounded. The Japanese were all but wiped out. It gave shocked Americans at home a foretaste of how fighting the Pacific war would be.

Operation *Flintlock*

Next in line were the Marshall Islands, which had been mandated to Japan after World War One and were seen as a perimeter defence to the home islands by the Japanese. The usual brand of Japanese fanaticism was to be expected as the US aimed for the first time to conquer Japanese soil.

A mighty invasion force was marshalled in Operation *Flintlock*, of some 85,000 personnel and nearly 300 warships, transports and landing craft. On 30 January 1944 the landings began on Kwajalein, the world's largest atoll. As many as 36,000 shells were fired on the atoll in preparation for the landings, shattering the established fortified positions. Resistance was consequently less than might have been expected. Nevertheless, before it was over some 8,400 Japanese lay dead compared with 500 Americans – half the number killed in the conquest of the Gilbert Islands.

The Japanese had moved men to the outer atolls in expectation of an invasion and the Americans knew this, thanks to the code-breakers who deciphered the Japanese signals. Bombs delivered from the air helped to neutralize these outer atolls and they were duly bypassed, although their defenders did not surrender until the end of the war.

By 23 February Eniwetok atoll was also in US hands. A timely attack on the Japanese forces at Truk, an atoll further to

the west in the Caroline Islands chain, undertaken for the first time with radar-guided night bombing closed the option of retaliation from this quarter for the Japanese. After the customary naval bombardment – on this occasion delivered from surprisingly close quarters by US battleships – the Marines swarmed over the atoll. Most of its 3,500 Japanese defenders were killed. Now a strategically useful airfield was in American hands.

This meant that any hopes the Japanese had of reinforcing Wake Island or the by-passed atolls were at an end. For the Americans there was also the luxury of a new, large and safe anchorage perfectly placed for the next stage of the campaign.

After the fall of selected Marshall Islands no others in the central Pacific would be targeted by American invasion forces. A mighty number were by-passed as the US sought out the strategic big fish to net. It was a savage but effective tactic. With supplies in jeopardy and now behind enemy lines, the defending Japanese garrisons on those islands were left to fend for themselves, a large number of whom starved to death.

The Marshall Islands, January - February 1944

American troops storm Japanese positions on Kwajalein.

CHAPTER EIGHT

The Marianas

*One of the most distressing scenes of the war
yet to materialize occurred on Saipan as Japanese
civilians threw themselves from cliff tops, often
with their children in their arms.*

The Marianas are a group of mountainous islands in the West Pacific ocean that include, among others, Tinian, Saipan and Guam. Small in size they may be, but, lying just 1,200 miles south of Japan, their strategic importance was immense. With the capture of the Marianas Islands the Americans would have control of an airbase from which they could strike Japan. The islands were also important to the Japanese as stopovers in a line of supply and communication between the home islands and the southern acquisitions. If this was disrupted it would mean another blow to the aspirations of the empire. As a matter of national pride, the US also wanted to restore Guam to its list of territories, having lost it suddenly to the Japanese in the rash of Japanese invasions following Pearl Harbor.

There were, however, significant diffi-

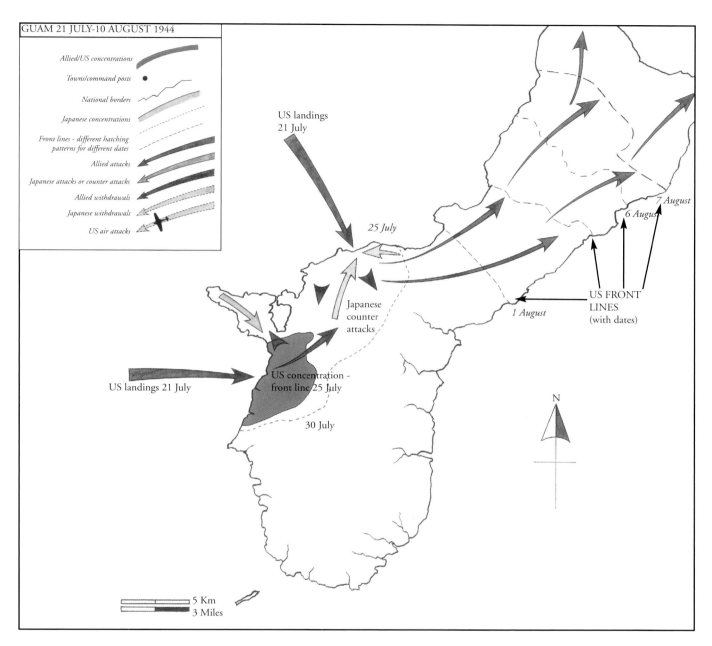

GUAM 21 JULY–10 AUGUST 1944

Allied/US concentrations

Towns/command posts ●

National borders

Japanese concentrations

Front lines – different hatching patterns for different dates

Allied attacks

Japanese attacks or counter attacks

Allied withdrawals

Japanese withdrawals

US air attacks

US landings 21 July

25 July

Japanese counter attacks

US landings 21 July

US concentration – front line 25 July

30 July

7 August

6 August

US FRONT LINES (with dates)

1 August

N

5 Km
3 Miles

culties to overcome. On Saipan, an important administrative centre for the Japanese, there was a sizeable civilian population. It was the first time the safety of civilians would play a part in US military planning.

Still, Operation *Forager* began in February 1944 with aerial attacks on installations. The landings were scheduled for 15 June.

The first target was Saipan for its proximity to the Japanese home islands. The US task force, comprising 800 ships and 28 submarines, left Majuro in the Marshall Islands on 6 June 1944, buoyed with news of the Normandy landings. It is staggering to appreciate that America was undertaking two major amphibious assaults concurrently, such was the might of its industrial output and manpower reserves.

But the battle for Saipan was bitter, and prolonged by Japanese intransigence. On 11 July Lieutenant General Yoshitsugu Saito, commander of the Saipan defences, sent a telegram to Tojo:

Marianas Islands, June-August 1944

US Marine uses flamethrower to clear out a Japanese bunker on Saipan.

'I have issued the following order: On (the day after tomorrow) we will advance to attack the American forces and will all die an honourable death. Each man will kill ten Americans.'

The Marines were reinforced by the US Army's 27th Infantry Division, and together they hounded the Japanese into a corner. On 7 July about 3,000 Japanese committed themselves to a banzai charge that – inevitably – ran out of manpower within 24 hours. By 10 July Saipan was secure.

One of the most distressing scenes of the war yet to materialize occurred on Saipan as Japanese civilians threw themselves from cliff tops often with their children in their arms. They were both shocked and shamed by defeat but also terrified by tales of American barbarism. Their route to the cliff top at Marpi Point was strewn with empty bottles of sake and beer. Troops who stood by made appeals via a loud speaker system but they could do nothing to dissuade the suicidal, nor could the native Saipanese who did everything they could to rubbish the fears of the Japanese. The waters below the cliff were smothered with the bodies of dead men and women with children strapped to them. By the time the distressing incident was over two out of every three Japanese civilians on the island had chosen to die.

By the time Saipan was in US hands in July 1944 a total of some 29,000 Japanese had died while there were 16,525 US killed and wounded.

The battle for Saipan also led to a certain amount of friction between the US Marines and the US army. In essence, the Marines felt the soldiers were too cautious regarding military enterprise. The result

was that the Marine commander, Holland Smith, dismissed the army's top man in Saipan, Major General Ralph Smith, to assume direct control of the operation. The issues were finally resolved in Washington by heroic attempts to smooth over the crisis.

Guam

On 21 July, the 3rd Marine Division and the 1st Marine Brigade of General Turner's Joint Expeditionary Force landed at Agat and Asan on Guam, north and south respectively of the Orote Peninsula. Once again, relatively easy landings were followed by tough, savage fighting against a fanatical enemy, well dug into the hillsides and rugged terrain of the island, and

determined to hold out at all costs. The Japanese troops fighting around Mount Alifan in the south had mostly been subdued by the end of July, while further to the north the 3rd Marines had fought their way across a whole range of mountain ridges to the maind town of Agana by the same date. The next week was spent pushing the front line back up to the extreme northern point of Guam at Machanao, against a Japanese resistance that was becoming ever more fanatical, as evidenced by the increasing number of the by-now familiar Banzai charges.

The Marines, supported by 77th Infantry Division, finally overcame most Japanese resistance by 10 August. As was by now becoming a grim routine, there were few prisoners, the 18,000-strong garrison preferring to sacrifice their lives rather than surrender. In some instances, the fight was taken to ludicrous extremes; the last Japanese soldiers on Guam, hidden in the rough ground of the north of the island, did not finally surrender until 1972, twenty-eight years later.

The Battle of the Philippine Sea

While the battle raged on Saipan, another was underway at sea. The Battle of the Philippine Sea during June was the conflict's biggest between carriers. The First Japanese Mobile Fleet commanded by Vice-Admiral Jizaburo Ozawa took on the Fifth US Fleet under the authority of Admiral Raymond A. Spruance.

The Philippine Sea

USS Bunker Hill *is near-missed by a Japanese bomb, during the air attacks of 19 June 1944. The Japanese plane, with its tail shot off, is about to crash, at left.*

The Japanese had hoped to destroy a third of the American craft with judicious use of its land-based aircraft and submarines. But its ambitions were thwarted when 17 out of 25 Japanese submarines were sunk and the airstrips earmarked for action were wrecked by bombing.

Initially, Ozawa still held an advantage because the Americans had no idea where he was in the Pacific. But when he broke radio silence to order aerial bombardments, the US fleet was able to send up sufficient aircraft to dismantle the attack. Only 130 aircraft out of a total of 373 returned to Japanese bases. Soon afterwards a further 50 Japanese aircraft were lost above Guam in an event known by

B-17 Bomber

of the USAAF on a bombing run over the Solomon Islands, preparatory to the US assault on New Guinea, October 1942.

Americans as 'The Great Marianas Turkey Shoot'. While this was occuring the Japanese lost the carriers *Taiho* and *Shokaku* to torpedo strikes.

Still the drama wasn't over. Task Force 58, under the command of Vice-Admiral Marc Mitscher, who had been captain of the USS *Hornet* from which the Doolittle raid was launched two years previously, set out in pursuit of the Japanese fleet and launched a carrier aircraft strike that took out the *Hiya*, a prestigious Japanese carrier and damaged two others. Hampered by lack of fuel and dark skies about 80 US aircraft got into difficulties on return, although most of their crews were saved. As for Ozawa, he had just 35 carrier air-

craft remaining. Spruance desisted from swooping on the remainder of the Japanese fleet out of duty to the invasion force at Saipan.

Nevertheless, the disaster for Japan was clear. While its fleet still had some substance the number of aircraft it could muster was pitiful, this in a war where air superiority was everything. On 18 July Tojo resigned as prime minister and war minister following intense pressure, particularly from the Royal princes and, indirectly, from Emperor Hirohito. Before his departure was publicly announced he made a final radio broadcast:

Our empire has entered the most difficult state in its entire history. But these developments have also provided us with the opportunity to smash the enemy and win the war. The time for decisive battle has arrived.

He left the studios to clear his desk in the chief government building.

But although the cautious Emperor managed to dispatch the military figurehead he was unable to change the conviction of the Imperial Japanese Army that its men should fight to the death. And, given Japan's perilous situation, there were few candidates for the post. A compromise was found in Lt General Kuniaki Koiso, acceptable to both the army and navy but given the job entirely on the basis that he worked by committee.

If the dilemma facing Japan was not clear to its inhabitants at the end of 1944, it certainly became so during the early months of 1945. Now that the US runways in the Marianas Islands were completed, devastating bombing raids against the home islands quickly became the norm.

On 4 February 1945 70 Boeing B-29 Superfortresses dropped 160 tons of incendiaries upon the city of Kobe. Most of its buildings were made of wood and they blazed instantly. Similar treatment was dished out to Tokyo on 25 February and 450 tons of incendiaries destroyed an estimated 28,000 buildings.

In March the bombers came at lower altitudes and at night for increased effectiveness. Firestorms similar to those seen in German cities such as Hamburg and Dresden ensued. People died by the thousand and the terror among the survivors was immense. Journalist Masuo Kato recalled his nehphew Kozo Ishikawa who:

...held an unshakeable faith in Japanese victory. To his small world it was unthinkable that the Emperor's armies could suffer defeat or that the Japanese navy should endure any fate other than glorious victory.
After his home was burned to the ground during a B-29 raid. Destroying almost every familiar material thing that had made up his existence, he told me with great gravity: "We cannot beat the B-29."
The psychological effect of the loss of his home went deep. He had been one of the happiest and most carefree of children. He became thoughtful and serious and it was seldom that he laughed. He became ill and died shortly after the war was over. A nervous breakdown, the doctor called it.

The raids continued throughout the spring of 1945. When Tokyo had been laid to waste, Major General Curtis Le May turned his attentions to other cities, frequently, dropping leaflets warning of an impending raid, further driving down morale among a hungry and increasingly desperate population.

Seek and Destroy

Japanese cargo ship the
Nittsu Maru *sinking in the*
Yellow Sea, off China, on
23 March 1943. Periscope
photograph, taken from
USS Wahoo, *which had*
torpedoed her.

The War Under the Sea

American submarines were also playing their part in the new wave of Allied victories in the Pacific. Japan was in a similar position to Britain, being an island nation and entirely dependent on imports for vital commodities including oil. For a while, German U-boats threw a stranglehold around Britain and that might have signalled the end of the conflict but for the timely successes of the code-breakers who were ultimately able to pinpoint the whereabout of the German submarines and nullify their effect.

Japan suffered in a similar way when American submarines gained supremacy in the Pacific. However, there is little evidence to suggest that the Japanese managed to crack the American codes, for the empire's shipping remained vulnerable to US torpedoes until the end of the war.

The US submarines were based at Pearl Harbor and Freemantle in Australia. Their targets were naval ships, particularly carriers, and merchant shipping in order to deprive the Japanese war machine of the raw materials it needed to continue. The statistics of success are breathtaking. As 1944 dawned the Japanese had the use of 4.1 million tons of merchant shipping, excluding tankers. By the end of the year this had been reduced by more than half. In September of that year some 700,000 tons of shipping transported oil about the empire. Four months later, the figure had been reduced to 200,000. By 1945 the supplies of oil reaching Japan were almost non-existent, rendering the home and war economies inoperable.

The Japanese also had submarines, but their use was far more restricted. Japanese submarines were responsible for some raids along the coasts of Australia and America but the triumph of these lay mostly in causing a dip in morale rather than significant damage. Otherwise they almost always kept within the shadow of the big naval ships while US submarines roamed independently or in packs.

Later Japanese submarines were used to transport men and supplies to the battlefront rather than striking at the enemy. During the war the US lost 52 submarines out of a force of 288 while the Japanese losses totalled 128 submarines from 200.

It hadn't all been a bed of roses for American submariners. At the start of the war a faulty torpedo design hampered their actions. By 1943 this was rectified and after that they kept themselves busy in Pacific waters. After mines were laid around Japan in May 1945 there were further catastrophic losses to the Japanese mercantile fleet.

CHAPTER NINE

The Battle of Leyte Gulf

The domino fall of Pacific islands after 1942, this time to the American forces, indicated that the result of the war was assuredly going to be in favour of the Allies.

Japan had declared the independence of the Philippines on 14 October 1943. As in other territories similarly placed the independence was nominal, trade was restricted and civil freedoms muted.

Eleven months after this 'independence' had been declared, US reconnaissance decided that the Japanese were present on the island of Luzon in the Philippines in much lower numbers than they had previously believed. The plan for a swift invasion was ratified by Allied Chiefs of Staff meeting at the time at the second Quebec conference and a previous plan to first occupy the more southerly island of Mindanao was scrapped. The invasion launch date was 20 October 1944. For better or worse, the Philippines would be liberated.

It was all a matter for personal rejoicing for General MacArthur, evicted ignominiously from the Philippines earlier in the war. MacArthur – who curiously shared an ancestor with both Roosevelt and Churchill – was concerned for a while that his promise to return to the Philippines might come to naught. The US navy was set on approaching Japan through the Pacific and by-passing the militarily non-essential Philippines, comprising 7,000 islands. But MacArthur would brook no opposition, won the backing of Roosevelt by promising him success in the ballot box with the recapture of the Philippines and set about detailed planning. There was work to do, though, before the Philippines campaign could get underway.

Supplies could still be delivered to westerly outposts of the empire as the Japanese still held a line of outposts between the home islands and the occupied East Indies, albeit in diminished quantities.

Consequently, the Japanese defending Peleliu, in the Palau islands in the approaches to the Philippines, put up a tenacious resistance to the Marines who began invading on 12 September 1944. The Americans believed the island to be lightly defended. And so it appeared when the troops poured on to the beaches. However, the Japanese had decided to wait until the landing was well underway before revealing their hand. In a week the US Marines suffered terrible casualties, with the 1st Marines ending up at half their combat strength. The killed or wounded in the 5th and 7th Marines accounted for more than four out of every ten men sent ashore. As for the Japanese,

US Troops

continue their advance across the Pacific island chains, 1944. This is Peleliu island, one of the Palau island chain in the approach to the Philippines.

some 12,000 had died. For the record, Peleliu measured just six miles long and two miles wide and was of questionable strategic value.

It was, however, another defeat for the Japanese, and meant the emperor's military men, having realized the US invasion plan in the Philippines was imminent, were in effect forced to rely on gambler's luck. They had to destroy at least some of the might of the US navy when they themselves had precious little left to lose.

The domino fall of Pacific islands, this time to the American forces, indicated that the result of the war was assuredly going to be in favour of the Allies. However, the chances of the Japanese surrendering remained slight in 1944.

Japanese troops kept fighting because of an ingrained respect for the divine person of the Emperor. With surrender came the certainty that the Emperor would be deposed by the victorious Allies, perhaps even killed. The Japanese people would surely be enslaved and it was this notion that prevented a Communist-style revolution on Japan's home islands and maintained a degree of popular support for the war.

At its disposal Japan only had the remnants of its once fine fleet and the lucky survivors of its air arm. Nevertheless, the aim was to band the best of the ships together and attack the ships disgorging men and weaponry on to the island of Leyte. To do so the first striking force split into two after leaving Brunei. One group led by Vice Admiral Takeo Kurita aimed to approach the target area from the north while another came up from the south.

In the second part of this double whammy one column of the Japanese navy led by Ozawa would tempt into action significant American ships that would then be too far distant to assist the invasion force at Leyte. The operation was called *Sho-Go* or Victory.

This was the plan and it might have been pulled off had not a couple of American stalking submarines, *Darter* and *Dace*, spotted part of the Japanese invasion force in the Palawan Passage. Unaware that there were submarines in the vicinity, Kurita had called a halt to the customary zig-zig progress of the Japanese ships to conserve fuel, making them an easy target. In the early hours of 23 October the US torpedos swiftly sank two heavy cruisers and badly damaged a third. When *Atago*, the flagship, went under Kurita himself was plunged into the sea, along with many of his immediate staff. This was the first of four actions that comprise the Battle of Leyte Gulf, none of which, incidentally, took place in Leyte Gulf itself.

In fact, it was not the end of the action. US submarines evaded the depth charges tossed out by the remaining navy ships but *Darter* came to grief in the shallows of the passage. After stripping and torpedoing the stricken submarine, the *Dace* began a slow, uncomfortable trip back to Brisbane manned by two crews rather than one.

The submarine attack had been a blow to the Japanese operation. Now they had to contend with the fact that the Americans were aware of their movements. However, the Japanese commander was entirely committed to the operation and felt compelled to continue. He was at least able to summon up some air support from Luzon for the strike by American planes that he knew would unfold in the morning.

Battle of the Sibuyan Sea

On 24 October came the first surface action in the Sibuyan Sea when aircraft from Task Force 38 (3rd Fleet) discovered Kurita's forces. A first wave of US aircraft were driven off by Japanese planes and anti-aircraft fire from the ships. Only eight of the US dive-bombers escaped the scene.

As Kurita knew full well, there were more air strikes planned by the Americans and these found considerably more success. Astonishingly the Japanese flag ships *Musashi* and *Yamoto* absorbed a series of torpedo and bomb hits during the first encounter yet sailed on in a measure of serenity. But as the bombardment became perpetual the *Musashi* was left limping. Finally the mighty ship slipped to the ocean bottom, the victim of 20 torpedoes and 17 bomb hits.

Kurita was shocked by the fate of his once-powerful fleet in this phase of the battle, as evidenced by the contents of a telegram that he sent to Tokyo:

'The enemy made more than 250 sorties against us between 0830 and 1530, the number of planes involved and their fierceness mounting with every wave. Our air forces, on the other hand, were not able to obtain even expected results, causing our losses to mount steadily.'

He reversed his course and, in doing so, persuaded the US pilots he was pulling out of the battle altogether, a premature assumption that led to near-disaster in the later stages of the battle.

Battle of Samar, 25 October 1944

American survivors of the battle are pulled from the water, 26 October 1944. Some 1200 survivors of USS Gambier Bay, USS Hoel, USS Johnston and USS Samuel B. Roberts were rescued during the days following the action.

was to execute the pincer movement and destroy the forces at Leyte Gulf, all of which had their guns pointing to shore. However, in the evening of 24 October one prong of the Japanese attack force encountered six US battleships – five of which had been at Pearl Harbor – four heavy and four light cruisers accompanied by destroyers strung out along the Surigao Strait. It was precisely where the Japanese ships had hoped to slip into the waters approaching Leyte. In the battle that followed the Japanese commander Nishimura was killed and his flagship *Yamashiro* was sunk. Numerous others were sent to the bottom or disabled. A second Japanese force intended to back up the first slipped away when its commander saw the devastation that had been wreaked by the waiting Americans. Only two ships in Nishimura's force survived.

The second prong under Kurita fared better, slipping through the San Bernardino Strait into the Philippine Sea under cover of darkness without being noticed. It was only a matter of hours away from action at Leyte and Kurita could hardly believe his good fortune.

Some 15 miles ahead lay six escort carriers, vulnerable prey to a battle group like Kurita's. Battle commenced off the island of Samar in the early hours of 25 October. He only retired after sinking two Allied escort carriers and three destroyers. Heroic attacks mounted by a small, undergunned force confused Kurita, already undermined by the loss of prized ships and this probably caused his volte face.

Had he stayed, Kurita might well have won the day, wrecking the largest amphibious force yet used in the Pacific. But he believed the force ranged against him to be greater than it actually was. His

Land-based Japanese bombers wreaked a revenge of sorts by hitting the carrier Princeton (in a different location) in addition to damaging a cruiser and five destroyers.

The feint drawn up by the Japanese navy colum led by Ozawa – to lure the 3rd Fleet away from Leyte – swung into action on 24 October. (Although the decoy force ultimately lost four carriers it did keep the flak from Kurita's fleet.) Halsey was fanatically keen on exacting revenge for Pearl Harbor and he eagerly took the bait. He decided against an initial suggestion to patrol the San Bernardino Strait, thinking Kurita was already on his way home.

Now all that remained for the Japanese

chance to open fire on the invading forces at Leyte was gone as was Japan's final hope of glory although Kurita made it back to Brunei unhindered.

Halsey didn't know what to make of the messages fired off in his direction when the Battle of Samar got underway. He believed he had the cream of the Japanese navy in his sights and was reluctant to withdraw before spilling blood. Ultimately he sent back a task force although it arrived too late to be of help. At the ensuing Battle of Cape Engamo, Halsey picked off four carriers and a destroyer.

As for the Americans, the inquest into the absence of a patrol in the San Bernadino Strait rumbled on for years. The Battle of Leyte Gulf was a success for the US and its maritime supremacy was now assured. But a command blunder left it a whisper away from being a costly catastrophe.

The Imperial Japanese Navy, once thought to be invincible, no longer had the capacity to protect the home islands from predators. The largest naval battle of all time, involving some 300 vessels and many more aircraft, was over, and the Americans were adjudged to be the winners. Moreover, no naval battle of its like would occur again. Naval ships remained important but primarily as mobile aircraft launchers.

Battle of the Philippine Sea, June 1944

Japanese aircraft carrier Zuikaku (centre) and two destroyers under attack by US Navy carrier aircraft, 20 June 1944.
Although hit by several bombs during these attacks, Zuikaku survived.

One Last Hurrah

Crew members of the sinking carrier Zuikaku *give a final 'Banzai' cheer after the Japanese Naval Ensign was lowered, during the afternoon of 25 October.*

Ships lost in the Battle of Leyte Gulf				
US			**Japanese**	
Light carrier:	Princeton		**Carrier:**	Zuikaku
Escort carriers:	Gambier Bay, St Lo		**Light carriers:**	Chitose, Chiyoda, Zhihi
Submarines:	Darter, Shark, Tang		**Battleships:**	Fuso, Musashi, Yamashiro
Destroyers:	Hoel, Johnston		**Heavy cruisers:**	Atago, Chikuma, Chokai,
Destroyer Escorts:	Eversole,			Maya, Mogami, Suzuya
	Samuel B Roberts		**Light Cruisers:**	Abukuma, Kinu,
Torpedo boat:	PT-493			Noshiro, Tama
Fleet tug:	Sonoma		**Submarines:**	I-26, I-37, I-45, I-54
			Destroyers:	Shimotsuki, Shiranuhi,
				Unranami, Wakaba, Yamagumo
			Oiler:	Jinei Marui
			Destroyer transport:	102

On the shore the invasion of Leyte had begun on 20 October. The assault forces were divided into two and ultimately fed 202,500 troops into Leyte from 500 ships. Within four days two important airbases fell to them although the runways were in a parlous state. It wasn't until 3 December that Marine F6F-3N Hellcat aircraft could be landed there to provide thereafter something approaching adequate air cover for the fighting men.

However, the garrison on Leyte was

being reinforced by the Japanese and soon the 15,000 defenders became 60,000, making it tough going for the Americans, who were further held up by seasonal rainfall. However, the Japanese were unable to turn the tide of Americans back into the sea, not least because they had limited means of getting more food, equipment or men. Naval action against supply ships sent from Manila meant the stores soon dried up. As early as mid November Yamashita conceded that Leyte was lost and that Luzon, the larger, neighbouring island, would soon be as well. His defensive actions did succeed in delaying the attack on Luzon, however, which did not take place until 9 January.

Clearly, the Americans would approach Luzon from Lingayen, the same place the Japanese had themselves landed.

As the American invasion fleet gathered they were subject to Kamikaze attacks, the attack of suicide pilots on enemy ships.

A Divine Wind

If the Battle of Leyte Gulf and the invasion of the Philippines brought a certain measure of military satisfaction to the Americans it also revealed to them a worrying new development that would make warfare with the Japanese all the more dangerous. Kamikaze flights had been used during the Battle of Leyte Gulf, in the action off Samar, after the aircraft took off from airfields on the Philippines. Now the use would be more widespread – and more frequent.

The word approximates in translation to 'divine wind' and refers to the adverse weather conditions – specifically a

A Divine Wind

Kamikaze pilots attend a final briefing by a senior officer before heading off on their one-way trip.

Kamikaze

Japanese Kamikaze plane burning on the deck of a US aircraft carrier, possibly the USS Enterprise, *c. May 1945.*

typhoon– that prevented Japan's conquest by Mongol warlord Genghis Khan in 1281. For modern warfare the divine wind needed the sacrifice of willing volunteers who would turn their plane and themselves into a powerful weapon by smashing into a ship or even a land-based target. The slogan was 'one plane, one warship'.

There is evidence to suggest that at least one pilot turned Kamikaze at Pearl Harbor when his plane ran low on fuel, proof that the notion was always advocated by the Japanese. In fact, the idea was not universally supported; Yamamoto in particular was squarely against the sacrifice of Kamikaze, believing it was bad for morale.

But when Vice Admiral Takijirio Onishi realized a vast US naval fleet was heading for the Philippines he knew it was time for desperate measures. If the Philippines fell then the next stop for the Americans would be the Japanese home islands. Dubbed 'father of the Kamikaze', he explained to his troops: 'There is only one way of channeling our meagre strength into maximum efficiency and that is to organize suicide attack units composed of Zero fighters equipped with 250 kilogram bombs, with each plane to crash-dive into an enemy carrier.'

Senior staff officer Captain Rikihel Inoguchi was among those listening. 'The Admiral's eyes bored into us as he looked around the table. No one spoke for a while but Admiral Onishi's words struck a spark in each of us.'

The first Kamikaze operation was actually in September 1944, contrived by a group of army pilots on the Negros Islands, and was a strictly unofficial affair. Two men were picked as pilots and their planes were modified to carry 100 kilogram bombs. After taking off they were never seen again, probably being shot down before achieving their goal. This was also the fate of the first Navy Kamikaze, Rear Admiral Masafumi Arima, who took off from Clark Fields on 15 October aiming for a carrier but failed to either complete his mission or return to base. But America's good fortune would not last.

Before peace was made some thousands – some estimates say 4,000 but others claim more than 7,000 – of Japanese pilots, mostly aged between 20 and 22 although some were as young as 17, flew one-way operations. By committing suicide other Japanese fighters acted individually to further the Japanese cause. According to Allied records the Kamikaze campaign claimed 34 escort carriers and a further 288 were seriously damaged. The death toll among the Allied servicemen numbered more than 3,000 and twice that amount were wounded.

The advent of the Kamikaze was a sign that Japan had given up the fight. No longer could it hope to replace downed aircraft or dead pilots in order to take on the superior Allied forces. Refusing to bow to the inevitable, the Japanese decided on the Kamikaze policy to expend the remainder of their fliers and planes in the most destructive way they could conceive. The most promising target was a carrier, preferably with its decks crowded with fully fuelled aircraft. However, many smaller vessels were hit or suffered degrees of damage while some Kamikaze planes missed their target altogether and hit the ocean.

The selection process for Kamikaze pilots was gruesome but not entirely callous. Only children and first sons were relieved of this arduous duty. Those that remained had the opportunity to opt out of the Special Attack Corps, as the suicidal squads were known. Many firmly believed in the notion of self-sacrifice to save the emperor and Japan, yet at the final moment still refused to enter the aircraft that would take them to their doom.

No matter how enthusiastically a Kamikaze embraced his task he was still chained into the cockpit and drugged before take-off to prevent the natural urge for self-preservation to kick in. Those committed to death hoped to bring a measure of glory to themselves and their family. Among their fellow pilots they were known as the Sons of Heaven, or even 'gods without earthly desires'. In his last letter, one wrote: 'When you hear that I have died after sinking an enemy ship, I hope you will have kind words to say about my gallant death.'

Each wore a white knotted scarf around their necks, a headband recalling one worn in the days when the warrior

Armour Arriving

US tanks roll ashore from LCTs (Landing Craft, Tank) on Lingayen Gulf Beach, Luzon, January 1945.

On to Manila

US infantry advance cautiously along the road towards Manila, past dead Japanese soldier (foreground).

mately the surrender of the emperor released the Kamikaze in waiting from his death oath. Onishi was among those who could not bear the public humiliation of defeat. He killed himself in the traditional manner of 'hari kiri', disembowelling by sword.

In the Battle of Leyte Gulf the number of Kamikaze attacks were comparatively few and their effect on the outcome of the campaign was nil. The intransigence of the Japanese defenders caused far more American deaths. After Leyte was captured the island of Mindoro where resistance was meek fell within a few days. But the major task of taking Luzon lay ahead and the Kamikaze threat became greater than ever. In one single day in 1945 sixteen ships were lost to Kamikazes. The cruiser *Australia* was hit five times in four days but remained in action. Landings began on 10 January at Lingayen Gulf following a typically intense bombardment from US ships parked up in Leyte Gulf.

Elsewhere the US navy was unmolested and spread out from the Philippines into the South China Sea in January, hitting targets as distant as Saigon and Hong Kong.

Strong Japanese forces on Luzon were attacked not only by Americans but also by Filipino guerillas who risked much to join a battle of liberation. In fact, when the fighting was over MacArthur had many of them imprisoned for what he believed to be left-leaning politics. MacArthur's plans were complicated by the existence of numerous prisoners of war held since the fall of the Philippines. His chief concern was to liberate the various camps before any Japanese backlash took place.

His arrival, however, was too late to

Samurai class dominated and a cloth stitched with the hair of a thousand women – thought to be lucky.

When Kamikaze attacks began in earnest they dealt some horrible blows to the Allies, although fuel shortages and wanton fear among the pilots often meant aircraft never reached their assigned targets. But their greatest military value was in the psychological fear that spread among servicemen awaiting the buzz of an aircraft overhead and the panic that occurred when one appeared. There would be no surrender by a Kamikaze pilot and no question of mercy.

Some Kamikaze returned to their bases if they could not locate their targets. On the face of it, a sensible use of man and machine. However, the option was not encouraged. One pilot who came back remembered being arrested and then punched in the face by his senior officer. To survive was shameful – although ulti-

save a number who were shipped off to the home islands before liberation.

The plight of prisoners of war transported from the Philippines by ship, subject to American air attacks, was pitiful. Two ships were sunk, and at least one other was serious damaged by a shell that killed dozens of prisoners penned in already appalling conditions below deck. The desperation of survivors mirrored that of the Japanese troops retreating through Burma after being routed at Imphal and Kohima and the measures they took to survive were also similarly heart-wrenching. They snatched food from the dying, levered blankets from dead men, stole shoes, begged their Japanese captors for favours. For the shipboard men the danger lay in freezing to death.

Their eventual destination was Kushu Island. Even after they were off-loaded the fighting was continuing in Luzon.

Manila was only cleared of Japanese forces with house-to-house combat. By the time the city fell to the US on 4 March 1945, 16,000 Japanese lay dead. It took several more months to clear the rest of the significant Philippine islands of Japanese defenders. It was not until 2 September, long after any realistic hope of victory had vanished, that Yamashita finally surrendered, along with about 50,000 men, all close to starvation.

Retaking the Philippines

US infantry move off their beachhead on Blue Beach, Luzon and into the island's interior, January 1945.

CHAPTER TEN

Kohima and Imphal

*'When you go home tell them of us and say
For your tomorrow we gave our today.'*

LINES ON THE FOURTEENTH ARMY MEMORIAL, KOHIMA, BURMA

Despite the setbacks they were experiencing in the region in 1944, the Japanese remained convinced India could still be theirs, perhaps not to govern outright, but very possibly through a puppet government. This was fertile ground to cultivate insurrection by the nationalists who were weary of Imperial rule but unable to force the British to leave. If Assam at least could be secured, the aerial supply of the Chinese army could be disrupted or even halted.

Accordingly, a planned thrust into India was given enthusiastic backing by Japanese military leaders. In March 1944 the Japanese Fifteenth Army, worth more than three divisions and numbering some 155,000, under the command of Lieutenant General Mutaguchi breached the Indian border and headed for Imphal and Kohima for a twin-pronged assault.

Operation *U-Go* began with the crossing of the Chindwin River and the most optimistic of the Japanese troops believed it would end in Delhi, their hopes reflecting the worst fears of the British.

Using oxen, mules and elephants and with each man loaded down with food and equipment the Japanese covered a distance approaching 200 miles on foot (it is

The Battle for Imphal

British 3-inch mortar detachments support the 19th Indian Division's advance along the Mawchi Road, east of Toungoo, Burma, March-June 1944. The mortar proved the most effective weapon in jungle warfare.

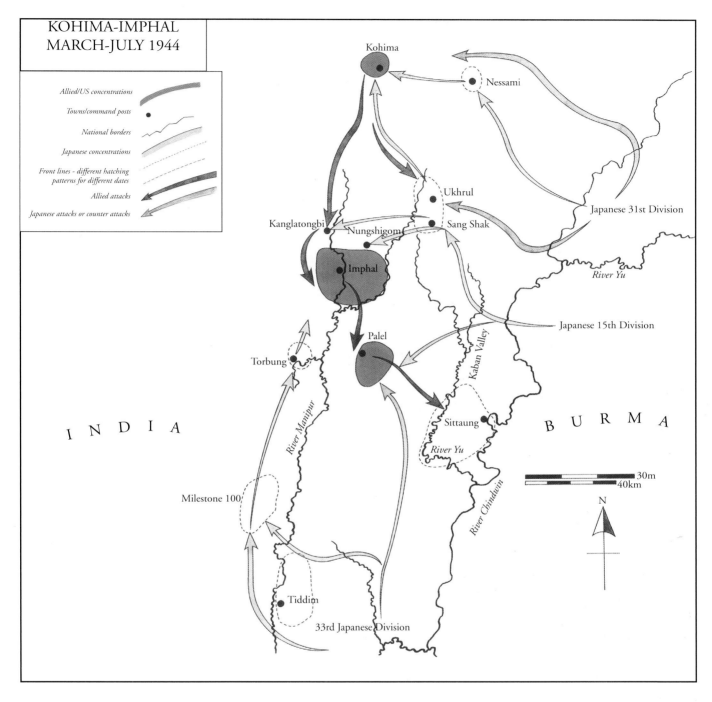

KOHIMA-IMPHAL
MARCH-JULY 1944

Allied/US concentrations

Towns/command posts

National borders

Japanese concentrations

*Front lines - different hatching
patterns for different dates*

Allied attacks

Japanese attacks or counter attacks

Kohima

Nessami

Ukhrul

Japanese 31st Division

Kanglatongbi

Nungshigom

Sang Shak

River Yu

Imphal

Japanese 15th Division

Palel

Kaban Valley

Torbung

River Manipur

I N D I A

B U R M A

Sittaung

River Yu

30m
40km

Milestone 100

N

River Chindwin

Tiddim

33rd Japanese Division

much shorter as the crow flies).

Mutaguchi was working to an ambitious blueprint which at least one member of his Army group, Lieutenant General Nobuyoshi, had branded 'a fool's enterprise'. But the Japanese were prone to outrageous optimism in military planning, firmly believing that one of their soldiers was worth at least three of the enemy's. Once again this ludicrous head-in-the-clouds thinking would prove their downfall.

Reinforcing Imphal

As for the Allies, victory had been secured in Arakan, so operations there were halted and, when Japanese intentions became clear, the British forces at Imphal were swiftly reinforced by the 5th Indian Division. They were joined by the

7th Indian Division and other stray brigades that could be pulled in, with even a brigade of Chindits pitched in to the battle.

Predictably, the invading Japanese were soon short of equipment as their supply lines were now long and subject to attack. About half the supplies earmarked for the Indian campaign never made it that far thanks to the work put in by British and American submarines, bombers and behind-enemy-lines saboteurs.

Mountbatten too was suffering from the effects of shortages, in his case of aircraft, until finally manaing to scrounge 79 transport planes on loan from the Mediterranean theatre to resolve the crisis.

The Japanese were supported in their attack by the Indian National Army, led by Chandra Bose and manned by enthusiastic nationalists and former Japanese prisoners of war who had once fought for the British empire. Despite a groundswell of opinion in India against the ruling British, Bose found it harder than expected to recruit support among Indians in Assam. The message that the Japanese were friends, not foes, did not seem to most Indians to ring particularly true. However, on 14 April 1944 the INA was able to hoist the Indian tricolor flag above Indian soil for the first time, some 28 miles (45 km) short of Imphal, when the invaders gained control of the region. (Bose went armed with new currency to tempt the loyalty of the locals.) Japanese artillery was firmly entrenched in the surrounding hilltops and pointing at Imphal. The stage was set for a titanic clash.

Who Controls Kohima, Controls the Pass

At Kohima, the British predicament was, if anything, even worse. Although it was something of a lofty outpost some 5,000 ft above sea level and 80 miles distant from Imphal, it was significantly sited above the Assam valley. Whoever controlled Kohima also controlled the pass through that valley, into the further reaches of India, as well as the railway links in the vicinity. Without Kohima, Imphal could not be held. Although they were braced for an attack at Imphal the British were not expecting action at Kohima, nor were they prepared for the speed at which the Japanese forces travelled.

Holding the defences were the 161st Indian Brigade, comprising the 4th Royal West Kents, 1/1st Punjabis and the 4/7th Rajputs, with a contingent of the Assam Rifles and Assam Regiment, with troops from the 5th and 7th Indian Divisions arriving by air to reinforce them later.

Remembering the Fallen

Veterans of the Fourteenth Army visit the grave of their former comrade Lance Corporal John Harman VC, awarded the Victoria Cross posthumously for gallantry at Kohima 8-9 April 1944.

Fierce fighting erupted between the British and Japanese as early as 23 March. Nevertheless, the Japanese managed to reach the outskirts of Kohima at 4 am on 5 April. The Japanese aim was to cut the links between Kohima and Imphal then surround the town from three directions. They were reliant by now on capturing supplies. A confident prediction that the battle would be won within 48 hours was turned on its head by the against-the-odds stubbornness of the defenders.

One of two Victoria Crosses awarded during the battle of Kohima went to Lance Corporal John Harman of the Royal West Kents for his brave exploits. Sniper Harman – who spent much of his boyhood on the remote Lundy Island in the Bristol Channel owned by his millionaire father Martin – sprang into action when he spotted a Japanese light machine gun team taking over a nearby trench.

Without hesitation he sprinted some 35 yards towards the trench, flung a grenade which killed the two Japanese inside and returned to his line bearing a captured gun.

Two days later on 9 April in cold, wet weather he repeated this astonishing performance only this time there were five men in the trench armed with automatic weapons and he himself used a fixed bayonet rather than a grenade:

When all the enemy were dead he walked back to his lines, ignoring his comrades' pleas to run for cover. He was killed by a burst of fire and died, saying 'I've got to go. It was worth it – I got the lot.

His actions kept the hill in British hands for the time being at least. A citation in the London Gazette on 22 June 1944 read:

Lance Corporal Harman's heroic action and supreme devotion to duty were a wonderful inspiration to all and were largely responsible for the decisive way in which all attacks were drive off by his company.

Legend has it that at the time he was killed the bees he cared for in a hive on Lundy all disappeared.

Pinned down in a trench nearby another soldier, H F Norman, witnessed Harman's actions and has left this description of the terrible conditions facing soldiers:

He (Harman) was covered by Sgt Tacon who was in a pit well behind us and could move about. He killed a Jap who was just going to throw a grenade at Harman. Harman killed the rest of the Japs but instead of running back as we were shouting for him to do he walked back calmly and the inevitable happened. He was shot in the spine by a Jap machine gun and was killed.

When Harman was committed to his final feat of courage another corporal next to Norman called Taffy Rees stood up in the pit and was hit twice, rolling into a no man's land. Another soldier who tried to rescue him was hit twice with bullets.

Norman explained:

Although we couldn't help Taffy we did start talking to him because he was only about two yards from us down in a dip but when he told us that he was paralysed we didn't think that there was much hope. He was soon delirious and for eight hours he was screaming, shouting and calling for his mum and dad and praying, until he died.
While he was lying there the company commander tried to get a smoke screen laid down so that Taffy could be evacuated by the

stretcher bearers but this proved unsuccessful. It was really nerve racking for the 14 of us left because we couldn't defend ourselves if we were attacked and would die 'like rats in a trap'.

The men finally withdrew after dark. Curiously Norman ends his memories of that terrible day with the words: 'I've had a hell of a headache all day today as well as a nasty cold.'

The unnamed heroes of the day included the local border tribesman, according to one commentator. Lieutenant Colonel R. King-Clark, writing a contemporary account of 'Assam Operations' carried out by 2 Battalion The Manchester Regiment between April and July 1944, praised the contribution of local Naga tribesmen. The Naga response to news that Japanese forces had crossed the Chindwin River in March 1944 was to mobilize as intelligence gatherers for Allied forces, although King-Clark hints that they would have been a formidable foe in their own right. He tells how they were 'physically very tough and brave…every family has its blood feud which could only be settled, up to not so very long ago, by taking the head of the enemy.' He continues:

Their ability to seek out and render valuable information about the Japs was of a very high order…the work they did in the hills and jungle as porters, stretcher-bearers and guides made possible many operations. Their loyalty to the British government and campaign has been exemplary…there is little doubt that…the opening of the Imphal Road would have taken a great deal longer without the help of the Naga tribesmen.

The Siege of Kohima

British positions at Kohima. The District Commissioner's bungalow, scene of heavy fighting, can be seen in the distance.

By 9 April the British and Indian defenders were isolated and a day later their Daily Issue Store and Field Supply Depot were being raided by the Japanese. By 13 April the chief battleground was the District Commissioner's bungalow and his tennis court, which became a treacherous 'no man's land', with each side firmly entrenched. Grenade combat was underway at virtually point blank range.

The battle diary of 4 Battalion Royal West Kents from 13 April gives us a glimpse of the frantic fighting taking place:

The Japs made a heavy rush attack at B Coy from the DC bungalow and succeeded in penetrating into a shed on a small but important hillock when a Bren (gun) jammed. The pln. Comd Lt King restored the situation by driving them out with grenades but not before the Bren gunner himself picked up a shovel and cracked at his assailants with it.'

Next day the diary notes another attack 'repulsed with many casualties to the enemy'. The defenders successfully received an air drop of water. But crucially the Japanese use of smoke bombs indicated that their stocks of ammunition were now running low.

The Japanese were also being pounded by artillery positions to the west of Kohima and shells were proving both accurate and devastating.

The defenders had been pushed on to a ridge and were attacked from all angles. For 16 days in April 1944 they held out, assisted by parachute drops and aerial raids on the enemy. Finally, on 20 April, relief came in the form of the 161st Indian Infantry Brigade fighting through from Dimapur with the 2nd British Division. The Japanese onslaught could not be sustained.

Tank driver Herbet Adderley with 149 Royal Armoured Corps recalled going

Advance

Men of the West Yorkshire Regiment and 10th Gurkha Rifles advance along the Imphal-Kohima road behind Lee-Grant tanks, March/April 1944.

Bunker Clearing

An Indian soldier using smoke grenades to clear Japanese troops from bunkers in the Maungdaw hills, during Fourteenth Army's advance, 1944.

into Kohima, driving a leading tank behind enemy lines. The crews of five tanks dispatched previously that day had all perished after the commanding officer had panicked. Adderley's tank was armed with a Thompson sub-machine gun that none of the crew had used before. The tank was soon hit by enemy fire:

The order to bail out came. I asked the gun loader to just open the door two inches so that I could see. He pressed the handle down, the weight of the door pulled out of his fingers and shot wide open. Christ Almighty. Two trenches of Japanese were about 100 ft away with their guns lined up on us. They were expecting us to come out of the turret where the commander would be. It gave us a few seconds. I pressed the trigger [of the submachine gun] but I could hardly hold it. It was going up and down like something

alive as it was difficult to hold but they dropped out of sight. I was out of that tank like a blue bottle fly and behind the tank. The rest of the crew was following.

Nearby they saw the body of the commanding officer:

I could not see any blood so I turned him over and his eyes started to flicker. He was in a dead faint. We grabbed his shoulders and made for the nearest tank. He was not the only one who could not overcome his fear, he was not the first and he was not the last.

Under the heading 'Crack On Everybody', King-Clark describes the successful advance from Kohima to Imphal, despite monsoon conditions and poor visibility. An abandoned operations order showed that Japanese commanders had intended to hold Maram for ten days, enabling their 31st Division to mount an orderly withdrawal. In fact they abandoned defensive positions inside 24 hours and – according to King-Clark – were routed. In his eyes one crucial component of the Kohima victory - the turning point of the war in Burma – was the performance of the regiment's Vickers MG (machine) guns which, he proudly notes, fired over a million rounds.

King-Clark went on:

'Many lessons had been learnt in the campaign, but perhaps the biggest one of all was that we had discovered we could beat the Jap at his own game, in his own type of country. The casualties throughout the Division were undeniably heavy but it was announced that since mid-April we had killed 3,800 Japs, which was several to one in our favour. All units of the Division now have a very much greater respect for, and confidence in, the Vickers M G than they had before the campaign began.'

Later Norman recalls how troops were airlifted to positions 20 miles beyond Kohima to conduct road patrols:

'By 1500 the Game was on. There was plenty of firing and we set fire to the bashers [field shelters] *which the Japs and Jiffs* [JIF: Japanese Inspired Forces. These were usually Indian Army or Burmese prisoners-of-war captured in previous campaigns and retrained.] *were in, then the side-show started. They started running from the bashers and our lads fired everything they had at them. I saw Jap bodies falling everywhere and piling up all over the area...when the bashers had burnt themselves out we found approx 70 Jap bodies.'*

It was the beginning of the end of Operation *U-Go* although the clearance of Kohima took some weeks. During this torturous time there continued to be sniper duels and grenades were hurled like snowballs. Once again, the savage fighting featured brutal use of the bayonet and flamethrower.

By now the Indian Nationalist Army and the Japanese were at odds, as Bose came to realize that the liberation of India was not at the heart of Japanese tactics. Fighting conditions were all the while horrific, particularly after the onset of the monsoon rains in May, as one veteran dispatched to help clear the Kohima outskirts relates:

'The physical hammering one takes is difficult to understand. The heat, humidity, altitude and the slope of almost every foot of ground combine to knock hell out of the stoutest constitution. You gasp for air which doesn't seem to come, you drag your legs upwards till they seem reduced to the strength of matchsticks, you wipe the sweat out of your eyes ... So you stop, horrified, to be prodded by the man behind you or cursed by an officer in front.'

Although the hopelessness of their situation was becoming increasingly apparent, the Japanese remained ardent combatants, weakened though they were by hunger and illness. As long as they had ammunition they would continue the fight. A major recalled the efforts by his company to rout out the invaders:

We were in Kohima for three weeks. We were attacked every single night . . . They came in waves, it was like a pigeon shoot. Most nights they overran part of the a battalion position so we had to mount counter attacks . . .

Water was short and restricted to about one pint per man per day. So we stopped shaving. Air supply was the key but the steep terrain and narrow ridges meant that some of the drops went to the Japs. My company went into Kohima over 100 strong and came out at about 60.

The second Victoria Cross recipient was Temporary Captain John Randle of 2 Battalion, The Royal Norfolk Regiment, who had refused to be evacuated even though he was wounded. On 6 May he led his men forward to capture a hilltop vantage point then saw that a neighbouring bunker remained in the hands of the Japanese. In the face of enemy fire he charged this bunker, threw a grenade inside and then flung his body across the opening, ensuring all inside would die.

In the air the Air Transport Command – comprising both the RAF and the USAAF – was at full stretch as crew and their ground support staff knew the lives of the men in battle depended on them. They never wavered although they were exhausted by their huge efforts. Also providing the Chinese army with supplies the air crews were veterans of flying 'over the hump', the Himalayan mountains otherwise known as The Aluminium Trail because it was so littered with wreckage. Airfields were poor, charts inadequate and weather conditions entirely unpredictable. Maintenance work had to be carried out in the comparative cool of the night as to touch the metalwork during the hours of sunlight was likely to cause second degree burns. Spare parts for planes were also hard to come by; most mechanics made do with cannibalised parts from other aircraft.

A UK Ministry of Defence estimate puts the number of tons of supplies delivered by the RAF during the battle of Kohima at 19,000. In addition it airlifted 12,000 men in, and 13,000 casualties as well as 43,000 non combatants out, as well as 14 million bags of rations, 1,200 bags of mail, 43 million cigarettes and one million gallons of petrol.

Lifting the Siege

By the end of May a withdrawal from Kohima was permitted by the Japanese high command. However, remaining troops were diverted to Imphal for what Mutaguchi called a 'do or die' assault. And the soldiers died in droves, not least for the want of decent supplies. Outraged, General Kotoku Sato, charged with fashioning the offensive, telegraphed his boss: 'The tactical ability of the Fifteenth Army staff lies below that of cadets.' He began a retreat to save the remnants of his forces. When Mutaguchi began to fire off some long range probing questions about the troop movements, Sato calmly cut the communications wires. He and two other divisional commanders were duly sacked, sending the morale of an already badly battered Japanese force further south.

The siege of Imphal was lifted on 22 June when the road between it and Kohima was finally free of enemy forces. The Allies now had the advantage of tanks while the Japanese had no anti-tank weaponry. Imbued by senseless notions of honour Mutaguchi refused to appeal to his superiors for a withdrawal. But by July the fruitlessness of the expedition was at last apparent and the Japanese pulled out of India. Even then the Japanese were compelled to fight for their survival without the benefit of air cover and they were pursued relentlessly both by Allied armies and airforces. Recollections by soldiers make grim reading. They fought one

On the Lookout

British soldiers search through long grass for Japanese snipers while covered by a Bren-gun team, Kohima area, 1944.

another for food, stripped walking boots from the sick and dying, they were drowned in great numbers by the swollen waters of River Chindwin. Pathways through the jungle were littered with debris cast off by the retreating Japanese. The most feeble were discarded in a similar manner, left to blow themselves up with grenades to prevent further torment or capture. The disaster cost Mutaguchi and his key staff members their jobs.

In human cost some 30,000 Japanese soldiers out of a force of 85,000 were killed. A further 23,000 were wounded. Sixty years later the names Kohima and Imphal still resonate with the memories of bitter, brutal combat, some of the worst ever seen in a war zone. Men on both sides were traumatized by thirst, hunger and tropical diseases. Malaria was rampant. There was also the mental anguish among Japanese, Indian and Allied soldiers caused by seeing comrades blown to pieces, and living under the perpetual threat of death.

Yet for the Allied soldiers there was some relief in terms of fresh water, food and medicines dropped by low flying transport planes and this proved the key to success. Apart from the drops that went astray, the supplies sent forward to the Japanese were sporadic to the point of being non-existent. At the end, the rewards for the victors were tremendous as the way was finally opened for an Allied operation that would win back Burma. There are numerous memorials at both Kohima and Imphal dedicated to those who died. Visitors are left to quietly contemplate the sacrifice as they read the words of John Maxwell Edmonds:

'When you go home tell them of us and say
For your tomorrow we gave our today.'

CHAPTER ELEVEN

Through the Central Hills

'Climbing mile upon mile of rough tortuous mountain track, pressing through deep, evil smelling mud, passing vile, stagnant mosquito ridden pools the stench of which sometimes overpowered us.'

<small>LANCE CORPORAL WILLIAM ELLIOT, EAST LANCASHIRE REGIMENT, ON THE CENTRAL BURMA ADVANCE</small>

The longest land campaign fought by the British in World War II was only half done when the battles of Kohima and Imphal were won. Now the task was to take control of each and every acre snatched by the Japanese after 1941 and it would not be completed until August 1945. Operation *Capital* was launched by Mountbatten to secure communications and supplies along the Burma Road.

Along that route lay Mandalay and the surrounding region, rich in rice fields and oil installations. If the Japanese were

River Patrol

Troops of the Fourteenth Army prepare to search a village for Japanese soldiers, during the advance through Burma to Rangoon, 1945.

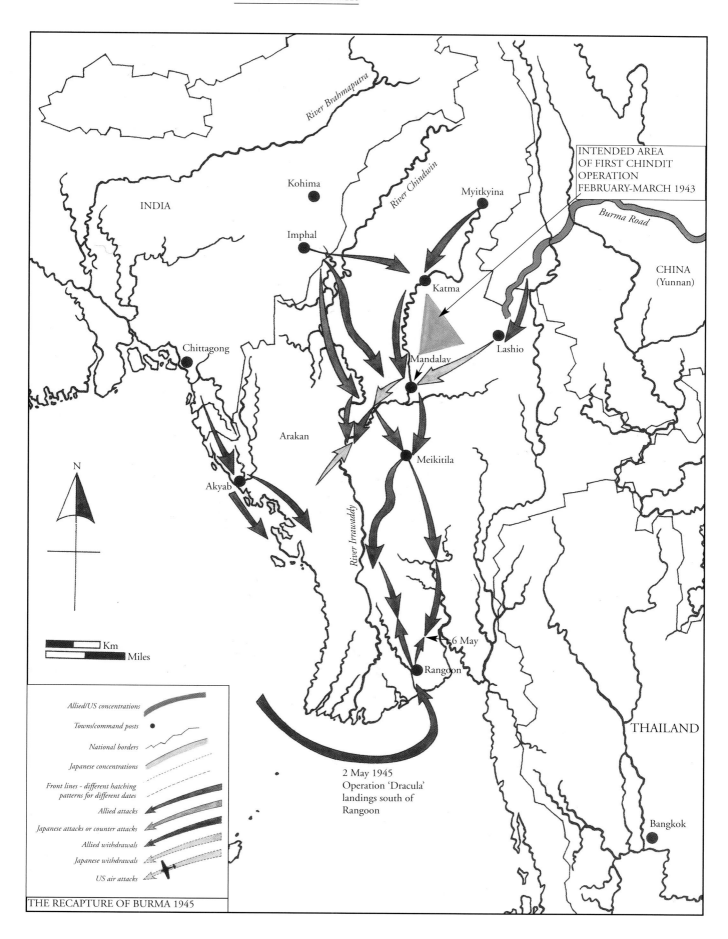

INDIA

River Brahmaputra

Kohima

Imphal

River Chindwin

Myitkyina

INTENDED AREA
OF FIRST CHINDIT
OPERATION
FEBRUARY-MARCH 1943

Burma Road

CHINA
(Yunnan)

Katma

Chittagong

Mandalay

Lashio

Arakan

Meikitila

N

Akyab

River Irrawaddy

6 May

Km
Miles

Rangoon

THAILAND

2 May 1945
Operation 'Dracula'
landings south of
Rangoon

Bangkok

Allied/US concentrations

Towns/command posts

National borders

Japanese concentrations

Front lines - different hatching
patterns for different dates

Allied attacks

Japanese attacks or counter attacks

Allied withdrawals

Japanese withdrawals

US air attacks

THE RECAPTURE OF BURMA 1945

deprived of these then their war effort would be severely curtailed.

Although the battle for Burma is remembered largely as a British show, those forces that began to forge through Burma with their sights set on victory were of a truly multicultural complexion. They included British, the Ghurkas, Indian, Burmese, Chinese, Black Africans and Americans, although the majority of the officers were British, and much of the planning was done by the Americans. Yet each ethnic division had its own motivation for fighting. A Chinese phrase sums up the situation well: 'same bed, different dreams'.

The British were keen to restore the extended boundaries of the empire carved out years previously in Queen Victoria's

time. Only the most far-sighted among the British could see that the days of imperial rule were numbered, that Britain's presence was largely unwelcome in the countries it garnered and that the age of nationalism was dawning to replace the tarnished era of colonialism.

Many Indians fought loyally for Britain during World War II in the ranks of the Indian Army. Out of one million troops under the command of South East Asian Command, created in August 1943, 700,000 were Indian. To state with certainty the driving forces of this immense array of Indian castes and creeds all standing under one umbrella is impossible. A great number more Indians fought on behalf of Britain rather than against the self-styled mother country yet it is

Guerrilla War

Patrol of American-led Burmese guerrillas crosses a river in central Burma, 1945.

doubtful they did so to further Imperial rule. Perhaps it was for no better reason than because it was customary to do so.

The Burmese were ethnically diverse and each group pictured in its mind a self-governing homeland for its people. Some groups supported the Allies in their fight against the Japanese. On 1 August 1943 Japan declared that Burma had its independence but in practical terms the declaration meant little. The Japanese were on Burmese soil in considerable numbers and they continued the (British) policy of taking the best for themselves. Had they given real government to the people of Burma, the Japanese might have won genuine support for their cause. As it was, the Burma National Army under the leadership of Aung San held together only until the British charge back into Burma appeared irreversible. Then there was rebellion and disarray. Many villagers were content to work for both the Allies and the Japanese, figuring life was much the same under both imperial powers.

For the Chinese the campaign against Japan was long-running and exhaustive. Japan had began squatting on Chinese territory since 1931, and open warfare had broken out between the two nations six years later. Most of China's industry and anchorage was now under Japanese control. Although Japan and its puppet governments did not have the broad support of the populace it did have air superiority, which counted. The Chinese themselves were divided between the nationalists led by Chiang kai Shek and the Communists under Mao Tse Tung and that hindered their effectiveness against the Japanese. Chiang courted the Allies primarily to get the necessary equipment and training for his men to win the domestic struggle against the Communists. At this stage in the war there was a certain economy exhibited by Chiang who wished to preserve as many stocks as possible for the civil war he knew would come. The Chinese also became infected with the belief that America would soon surround Japan and win the war and that little further effort by themselves was required. However, they were prodded into action primarily by the Americans who felt they had invested much into China during the war years and now wanted to see some returns.

From 1942 Chinese forces commanded by Chiang were trained by American General Joseph Stilwell, an expert in the Chinese language at a time when there were few. No fan of Chiang – whom he disparagingly nick-named 'Peanut' – or for that matter the British, he nevertheless fashioned a modern army with a will to fight that against general expectation made a considerable difference to the Burmese campaign. Stilwell, who marched out of Burma in 1942 at the head of his men after conceding 'we got a hell of a beating', was determined to lead his forces to victory there by way of revenge for the humiliation inflicted. Roosevelt's unstated aim was to keep China in the conflict and thus tie up significant numbers of Japanese troops that would otherwise be free to join the Pacific campaigns.

Black African soldiers were another product of the colonial days that Britain had hitherto enjoyed, coming from British East Africa and British West Africa.

Proportionately few Americans were involved in Burma. Most of those that were served under Major General Frank D. Merrill in the US 5307th Composite Unit, although they were known at home

'Uncle Bill'

General William Slim, Commander of the Fourteenth Army in Burma, Slim was one of the outstanding generals of the Second World War on any side.

them was General Claire Chennault, who had been training fighter pilots in China since 1937. The Flying Tigers, as his handpicked force was known, claimed an estimated 300 Japanese planes as they tried to keep the Burma Road, a vital supply link, out of enemy hands.

By March 1943 air strength in China was sufficient to form the 14th Air Force and Chennault was put in charge. His leadership was marred by a catastrophic clash with Stilwell.

Supreme commander of SEAC was Lord Louis Mountbatten, a great grandson of Queen Victoria and a bon viveur, who had undergone a chequered career in the navy but nevertheless ended up on top of the pile in Churchill's eyes. An accusation that the disastrous 1942 raid on Dieppe which cost thousands of Canadian lives was carried out at his behest to satisfy his mighty personal ambition failed to stain his record.

A fundamental lack of judgement meant that none of the operational suggestions he made were carried out in Burma. However, he did contribute significantly to the campaign in three areas. He ordered that fighting be continued during the monsoon season – and that had grave consequences for the Japanese army under Mutaguchi retreating from Imphal in June 1944. He insisted on more rigorous anti-malarial measures being taken. That entailed spraying the breeding areas with DDT, the daily administration of anti-malarial drugs by soldiers and conducting an education programme that highlighted the importance of taking basic hygiene measures. The results were astonishing. The incidences of malaria fell by almost two thirds between 1943 and 1945. (Research among captured Japanese revealed their knowledge of tropical dis-

through the columns of the press as Merrill's Marauders. Among the 3,000 men in three battalions were Sioux Indians and Japanese Americans. The codename of the unit was Galahad and it mostly fought alongside the Chinese.

America also fashioned its own long range penetration force, known as the Mars Task Force. Initiated in India in the summer of 1944 it comprised 612th (US) Field Artillery battalion, 124th (US) cavalry Regiment, 1st Chinese Regiment and the 475th (US) Regiment, including some men from Merrill's Marauders.

There were also American fliers who played key roles in supplying the troops aiming to reclaim Burma. In charge of

eases and steps to counteract them were still in infancy.) He also took steps to improve the flagging morale of troops, infinitely helped here by a string of Japanese defeats.

Working under Mountbatten was General Sir William Slim, known to his men as 'Uncle Bill', and one of the outstanding generals on any side of the Second World War. Although Slim once ruefully remarked, 'I must have been the most defeated general in our history,' referring to the resounding defeat the Indian Army experienced as it was chased out of Burma, he was the inspirational force behind the British Burma campaign. Now he was thoroughly committed to winning Burma back. His bulldog face continually inspired confidence in the troops and he could talk to most under his command in the Fourteenth Army in their own tongue, having mastered Urdu and Gurkhali.

There was no doubting the desire to oust the Japanese from south-east Asia although in truth Britain would have preferred to snatch back Singapore to patch up its imperial pride in the region before embarking on any other operations.

The Americans had different ideas, particularly given the declared US commitment to support China. The US wanted Burma opened up again to facilitate overland supply runs to China so they were no longer dependent on shipping in equipment by air across the Himalayas. The Ledo Road was forging ahead for that reason built by local labour and Seabees in the wake of Chinese and American forces heading east as an alternative to the Burma Road.

If the reconquest of Burma had to be next on the agenda the British would have chosen to do it from a southerly direction,

retaking the capital Rangoon with a seaborne assault. Once again British ambitions were frustrated. The demand for invasion craft elsewhere in the world meant a thrust from India across the Irrawaddy River was the sole option.

Chiang was unwilling to mount an offensive in Burma when the Japanese were still on his home territory. He had been reluctant to commit troops to the battles at Kohima and Imphal, believing the drama would unfold regardless of the presence of Chinese forces. Roosevelt thought differently, and prompted him into action with the implied threat that American aid would cease if no action was forthcoming:

. . . to me the time is ripe for elements of your Seventy-First Army Group to advance without further delay and seize the Tengchung-Lungling areas. A shell of a division opposes you on the Salween. Your advance to the west cannot help but succeed. To take advantage of just such an opportunity we have during the past year been equipping and training your yoke force. If they are not to be used in the common cause our most strenuous and extensive efforts to fly in equipment and to furnish instructional personnel have not been justified . . .

Chiang was duly chastened but his instincts were proved correct, however, for while the manoeuvres around Kohima and Imphal continued the Japanese mounted their final major offensive of the war against eastern China. The Ichi-Go operation began in April 1944, although it was not linked to Mutaguchi's exertions in India. Among its primary targets were the airfields of the south east which US planes used to launch harassment cam-

The Road to Rangoon

British and Indian Troops of the Fourteenth Army in Burma, advancing on Meiktila, 80 miles south of Mandalay, March 1945.

paigns against the Japanese in the Pacific. Despite the staunch resistance put up by some parts of the Chinese army the Japanese made swift progress, primarily because bitter political rivalries undermined the nationalists.

Although Stilwell was nevertheless determined to carry the Chinese with him into Burma. His ambitions were thwarted in October 1944 after Chiang used his influence to have Stilwell recalled.

The politics, allegiances and ambitions of all those heading across Burma under the Allied banner were many and various.

The aim, however, was the same.

In northern Burma Merrill's Marauders, the Chindits and the five divisions of Chinese troops captured the airfield and town of Myitkyina in the summer of 1944, revealing remarkable fighting spirit in the process.

On the Arakan flank two West African divisions took control of the Japanese communications centre of Myohaung before the end of January 1945. The pursuit of what remained of the 54th Japanese division through the Arakan was undertaken by 3rd Commando Brigade.

In central Burma Slim had the twin objectives of Mandalay and Rangoon. One of the first major obstacles faced by the troops was the massive Irrawaddy River, already traversed by the bulk of the Japanese.

Slim decided to seize back the initiative by establishing fake bases and phoney river crossings along a 200-mile stretch to confuse the Japanese. By the time the genuine river crossing occurred, at 4 am on 14 February 1945, an artillery barrage and aerial bombing put paid to Japanese resistance virtually before the Fourteenth landed on the southern shore. They struck up an impressive pace through the difficult terrain, keeping the Japanese on the back foot. Slim finally confronted the beleaguered remnants of the Japanese Fifteenth army in a pivotal battle south of Mandalay at Meiktila in a four week battle to finally nail the self-styled 'defeated general' name tag.

A counter-attack by reinforcements led to Slim's men being cut off for a while. However, a fresh brigade was flown in to ease the difficulties faced by the 17th Indian Division and the 255th Tank Brigade. His victory all but cleared the path to Rangoon.

Alf Turner was posted to the Far East in 1943 as a member of 6th Battalion, The Devonshire Regiment. He has clear memories of the dilemmas confronting British soldiers fighting in Burma:

All you can see around you in the jungle are trees, If somebody fires, you don't know which way it is coming from. Being a country boy I found it a bit easier than the Londoners out there who weren't used to night time noises and wildlife.
The Japanese soldiers would shout out in the night: 'Tommy, where are you?'

And they would beat bamboo sticks to unnerve us. They tried to get us to give away our positions.
After one attack an apparently wounded Japanese soldier was calling: 'Tommy, help me help me.' One of our officers who couldn't stick it any more went out to him. We told him not to go. When he got near the soldier jumped up and threw a grenade at him. The officer lost his leg.

Along with fellow members of B company Lance Corporal William Elliot from the 2nd Battalion, the East Lancashire Regiment, was flown to Myitkyina on 7 August 1944 where he witnessed evidence of the Japanese agonies:

Marched along a road which in places was strewn with bodies and parts of bodies of Japanese troops, where the ground had been blasted by heavy bombs and huge craters forced us to deviate from time to time from our course. The smell of decomposition was sickening and the sight of these mangled pieces of human anatomy appalling . . .

Later his journal recorded the problems encountered by the British soldiers. His descriptions are made all the more poignant by the lack of punctuation:

The long weary marches under the pitiless sun when the sweat from our bodies soaked through our battle dress and dried on the surface, leaving only a white salt deposit, while from our heads it ran into our eyes, stinging and blinding, coursed down our cheeks and was licked from our lips by parched tongues which thereby became even drier, our blistered and bleeding feet, legs stiffened by marching, so that when after a halt we had great difficulty in getting into stride again, our rifles and tommy guns

Enemy Armour

British officers inspect Japanese tankette, captured in the fighting around Imphal.

weighed on our shoulders and the slings bit into our flesh and our packs seemed to be boring a way into our back util they became a living, painful part of us, climbing mile upon mile of rough torturous mountain track, pressing through deep, evil smelling mud, passing vile, stagnant mosquito ridden pools the stench of which sometimes overpowered us, fording swift flowing chaungs with the water often breast high and then continuing our march with sodden clothes which clung to our legs and slowed us down while our boots squelched at every step until we began to wonder whether the coolness of the water on our burning feet and perspiring bodies had been worth the discomfort that inevitably folowed for the sun seemed to double its heat and our feet more readily blistered. How we longed for the iced drinks of Poona and dreamed of long copious draughts of iced beer such as we knew in Durban or the Knickerbocker Glories of Bombay, only to come down to earth and sip two or three drops of tepid brackish water from our bottles which for a short time would ease the harsh dryness of our mouths and throats. I can taste now the soap flavoured tea we often drank when water was too scarce to allow us to rinse our cups after shaving.

Most of us I am sure latterly began to feel that the war would never end, our loved ones and our country seemed to be in another world, long, long past and almost unreal. Only the jungle was real, the unending struggle and purposeless existences, it was something to marvel at that we were able to speak civilly and even jocularly to one another throughout.

Such, then, was the nature of the difficulties to be overcome by the Fourteenth Army on their long march through the jungles of Burma back to Rangoon.

CHAPTER TWELVE

Recapturing Rangoon

After the hellish road to Rangoon, the capture of the city was almost anti-climactic; when a division from XV Corps stormed the city, they discovered the Japanese had withdrawn.

The operation to regain Rangoon, code-named *Dracula*, involved amphibious and airborne assaults by XV Indian Army Corps under the direction of General Sir Philip Christison.

By the time the Allies had Rangoon within their sights, the most resistance they faced was coming not from Japanese troops, but from the weather.

The monsoon season was pending and a cyclonic storm only narrowly missed six convoys of troop ships and landing craft as they approached attack positions off Elephant Point.

The prospect of poor weather was always in the forefront of planning. Military planners knew if the assault did not take place promptly in March, it

The Burma Road

Clearing away a landslip on the Burma Road. The road is 726 miles long, often only 9ft wide, and joined Chungking, the wartime capital of China, to a railway terminus at Lashio.

would have to be postponed until November. In the end the progress of the Allied forces was so quick that to halt Operation *Dracula* would have been to lose a terrific momentum.

Royal Navy Captain H. W. Emerton was Staff Officer Bombardment attached to the 26th Indian Division HQ during Operation *Dracula*. His role was to advise on naval support, utilizing a battle group of cruisers, carriers and destroyers assembled at the mouth of the Rangoon River.

In his memoirs, written some time later, Emerton recalled the words of its commander, General William Slim: 'If we did not take Rangoon we should, with landing grounds out, even [air] dropping hazardous, roads dissolving and health deteriorating, find ourselves in a desperate situation with the prospect of a disastrous withdrawal…The possibility that alarmed me most was that the Japanese would, as they had in other towns, put a suicide garrison into Rangoon that would keep us out for the monsoon.'

The dilemma facing the military poised to take Rangoon was also a troubling one for different reasons. It was widely known that there were numerous Allied prisoners held in camps there. The risks to the internees during the city's invasion were through friendly fire and Japanese retribution.

However, the amphibious force – a division from XV Corps, a regiment of tanks and a Gurkha parachute battalion – stormed ashore to discover that the Japanese had gone. 'Only a few snipers were found in the city and these were rapidly dealt with,' observed Emerton.

In fact, it was prisoners who helped speed the invasion by daubing a message on their camp building roof, saying that the Japanese had gone. Following concern at the rapid progress of the overland Allied forces, the city had been abandoned and was there for the taking. This welcome message was spotted by a pilot in a low flying aircraft and consequently the invaders moved into the city unopposed.

But from here soldiers had to wade rather than march forward. Vehicles ground to a halt wheel-deep in thick mud. Men on both sides were constantly wet to the bone and as such were more prone to disease and the unwanted attentions of tropical creatures than ever before.

Christison had the task of mopping up the rest of Burma and was charged with chasing out the Twenty-Eighth Japanese Army, comprising two divisions, as it moved towards the east and Sittang. With the monsoon season in full swing the British units counted themselves fortunate to make half a mile each day. Conditions were, however, far worse among the Japanese forces who were compelled to abandon all transport and any weapons over 75 mm.

Christison later recorded:

Now to the rain and mud, malaria, dysentery and tick-typhus was added the outbreak of typhus and cholera. And hardly had this outbreak occurred when the plague struck. Cut off from all drugs and medical supplies, weakened by months of fighting and marching, men died like flies in large numbers. [The Japanese commander] took immediate steps. All men showing symptoms were collected in the rear of the division and left to die or recover.
All this time our plan was to avoid pitched battles, cut off as many as we could and let the monsoon and disease do the trick. All the time our artillery was given targets by the RAF and the Japanese lost heavily from this shelling.

The infamous bridge over the River Kwai, Burma.

The official British history of the battle in July 1945 further describes the misery of the Japanese:

By day the Japanese lay concealed on small, floating islands that dotted the swamps and at night floundered through the morass often up to the neck in water, feeling for a foothold in the inky water. Losses were heavy, there was no food and exhausted men sank out of sight, their comrades too weak to help them. Many went mad, others...wandered west again. Only those of the highest morale and fitness ever even reached the Sittang.

It was the last land battle fought by the Japanese; the final action of the Second World War. And it was prolonged by a Japanese refusal to believe that there had been an armistice: not until the RAF dropped leaflets over Japanese positions in August were the troops convinced that the conflict was finally over.

In two months a Japanese army had been wiped out. Out of a total of 27,000 fighting men just 7,000 escaped. The total number of Allied casualties in the same period stood at 95.

The war in Burma between 1941 and 1945 was fought in appalling conditions. The loss of life on both sides was huge and the commitment to victory from an assortment of races and creeds was admirable. But Burma was something of a sideshow to the main event. Victory there redeemed some lost pride for the Allies. However, it did little to secure the ultimate triumph over Japan in 1945. America had the necessary airfields to carry out bombing raids on the Japanese home islands. Indeed, the American generals were so confident of the likelihood of victory by 1944 that they bypassed Formosa (Taiwan) as they island-hopped towards the empire's heart. Unpalatable though it seems for those who took part, had the Japanese held fast in Burma the outcome would still have been the same.

CHAPTER THIRTEEN

Iwo Jima and Okinana

As the Marines came ashore on Iwo Jima, they were greeted with a bare, charmless island whose scrub vegetation would offer them no cover at all.

For the Americans seeking a new toehold closer to Japan, the island of Iwo Jima was an obvious choice. The purpose of its invasion, by Allied reckoning, was threefold. Lying just 650 miles from Tokyo, it was the first traditionally Japanese territory to be targeted and its fall would mean a shocking psychological blow to the enemy.

More crucially still, it possessed two airfields from which air raids on Japan could be launched. While the air strips in the Marianas were welcome additions to the US aerial war against Japan, mounting raids from them was proving expensive because they were so distant from the home islands. Also, no Allied fighter planes could provide the necessary protection as they simply did not have the fuel capacity for a 2,800 mile round trip. A happy by-product of the occupation of Iwo Jima would be that Kamikazes could

Liberators over Iwo Jima

USAAF B-24 'Liberator' bombers fly a sortie over Iwo Jima, the penultimate US conquest in the Pacific.

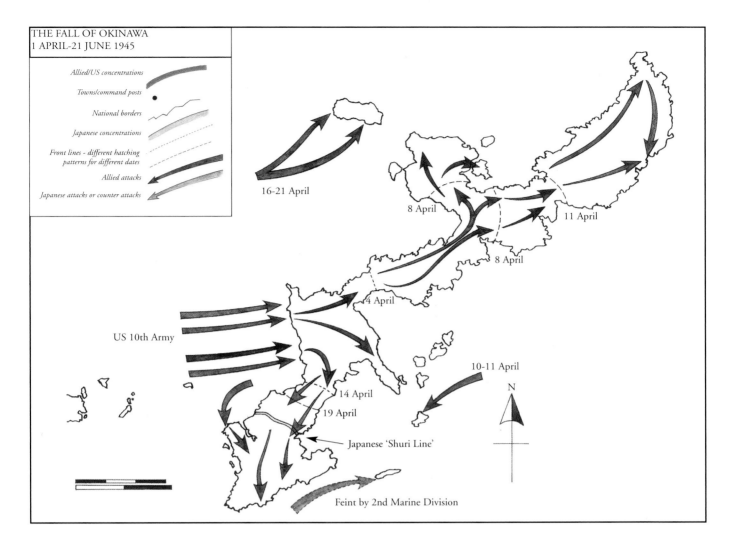

THE FALL OF OKINAWA
1 APRIL-21 JUNE 1945

Allied/US concentrations

Towns/command posts

National borders

Japanese concentrations

Front lines - different hatching
patterns for different dates

Allied attacks

Japanese attacks or counter attacks

16-21 April

8 April

11 April

8 April

4 April

US 10th Army

10-11 April

N

14 April

19 April

Japanese 'Shuri Line'

Feint by 2nd Marine Division

no longer use the air strips for their final flights towards major ships. The final pressing reason for taking Iwo Jima is that it and the rest of the Bonin Islands provided a natural northern defence of the Marianas Islands.

The Japanese Dig In

These sound strategic reasons proved scant consolation to the Marines charged with taking Iwo Jima. Packed into landing craft on 19 February 1945, a most unprepossessing sight greeted them of a bare island devoid of charm whose scrub vegetation would offer no cover to invading forces. The island, just five miles long and half that distance in width, was packed full of Japanese veteran fighters who had

been instructed to fight to the death. The Japanese military had correctly identified US plans to take Iwo Jima, appreciating its tactical advantages, and had given ample consideration to the island's defences, shipping in extra manpower.

In preparation, the Japanese had dug in deep – the soft volanic rock that the island was made from was ideal for the purpose – and tunnelled ferociously. One of the labyrinths was 75ft deep, had a dozen different exits and could hold 2,000 troops. Installed in prominent positions was an armoury comprising heavy and medium artillery, anti-aircraft batteries, heavy and light machine guns, mortars and tanks together with substantial quantities of ammunition. Island defenders knew that

Storming Iwo Jima

US Marines of 4th Division take cover from enemy fire on the shores of Iwo Jima, 19 February 1945. A US battleship and amphibious vehicles are docked on the beach.

every day they held out postponed the aerial bombardment of Tokyo, where many had family. In letters home the soldiers wrote about their impending death

For several months before the February invasion the island was bombarded by carrier aircraft and from off shore by the big naval guns. With the defending Japanese relatively safe in their underground network, the results from the US perspective were disappointing.

An armada of 450 ships of the US 5th Fleet assembled off Iwo Jima on the morning of the invasion. A total of 482 assorted landing craft brought the men of eight US Marine battalions ashore, with the first wave hitting the beach at about 9am.

Progress up the beach was surprisingly problem-free for the Marines. True, the men were weighed down with heavy packs that made scrambling through the steep slopes of unstable volcanic ash on the foreshore a challenge. But the onslaught that was expected did not occur.

Only when they broached the first sand ridge did a hail of Japanese bullets cut into the men, felling them in droves. Trying to make sense of the lessons learned on Saipan and Guam, the Japanese commanders were resisting the urge to man pill boxes that made easy targets for attacking aircraft. Instead they'd secreted themselves in caves and used sniper fire with the express intention of killing ten Americans for every Japanese soldier. The Japanese used their geographical height advantage to great effect, causing devastation to the initial waves of men. With considerable courage those men continued over and through the Japanese defences in order to permit the landing operation to continue unfolding behind them. Thanks to that astonishing determination some 30,000 Marines were ashore by the end of the day, already outnumbering the Japanese. On that first day 566 US Marines were dead or dying.

The night brought no respite for the Marines who, hemmed in to a small beachhead, remained under almost perpetual fire. There were no banzai charges by the Japanese who were by now intent on defence. Americans found these customary all-out charges easy to counter and possibly underestimated the strength of the garrison at Iwo Jima. Naval and aerial ordnance rained down, sometimes only feet away from the troops it was meant to protect. It was by any standard a fearful bloodbath.

As the battle became drawn out the Japanese were increasingly troubled by flies, cockroaches and a lack of fresh water. They were also compelled to conserve ammunition as best they could, making sure that each round counted.

Raising the Flag

Iwo Jima is fixed in modern consciousness for two reasons. Firstly the invasion was the subject of a film made in 1949 called *The Sands of Iwo Jima* that contained authentic combat footage and for which actor John Wayne won an Oscar nomination. Secondly, a picture by news photographer Joe Rosenthal of men under fire raising the US flag won a Pulitzer prize and later was turned into a huge sculpture dedicated to the memory of those who died.

In fact, Rosenthal had captured a re-run of the incident. On the morning of 23 February Marines from Company E in the 2nd Battalion survived the treacherous climb to the top of Mount Suribachi, an extinct volcano that at 550ft is the highest spot on Iwo Jima, to raise a small Stars and Stripes. (The Japanese had been pinned underground by naval and aerial bombardments.) Within two hours, when enemy presence on the slopes had finally been eradicated, a larger flag some 8ft long taken from a tank landing ship was installed by five Marines and a navy hospital corpsman and it was their actions captured on camera by Rosenthal. Three of the six men in the picture later died on Iwo Jima.

Later sculptor Felix W. de Weldon, attached to the US Navy, made a larger than life-sized model of the scene. He even tracked down the three survivors – Pfc Rene Gagnon, Pfc Ira Hayes and PhM 2/c John Bradley – so he could properly model their faces. After years of work the statue with 32ft high figures and a 60ft long flagpole was dedicated by President Dwight Eisenhower on 10 November 1954, marking the 179th anniversary of the US Marine Corps.

Later Bradley told how pipes used for water transportation by the Japanese were ripped up for the flag pole. His war continued virtually immediately the flag was aloft, as the task of flushing out the Japanese from the honeycomb of tunnels now literally beneath their feet continued:

After the flag was raised we went back to work taking care of the Japs that were here and there and we found many of them in caves. In fact in one cave we counted 142 Japs. And the flame throwers did a fine job on top of the mountain. We tried to talk them out. They wouldn't come out so then we used the flame throwers as a last resort. There were numerous caves all around there and

Planting the Flag

US Marines plant the 'stars and stripes' on the summit of Mount Suribachi. This was not, strictly speaking, the first 'raising of the flag' but a re-enactment for photographer Jack Rosenthal. The image became a defining image of the US victory in the Pacific, however, there was a lot more fighting to be done even on Iwo Jima, before the Japanese finally surrendered.

we didn't have one single casualty on top of that mountain.'

Flame throwers had first been used by Germans in World War One. By now they were a regular weapon for the Marines invading the Pacific islands. The weighty gas tanks were strapped to the back of the operator who directed a 20-40 yard jet of napalm into caves containing enemy fighters. In doing so they could hear an initial scream from the victim but death from suffocation, burns or shock was only a few seconds away.

Even after the flag was raised the battle raged on. On 12 March Bradley was injured on Iwo Jima when a mortar shell exploded near him. He was one of 19,200 wounded before Iwo Jima was secured while about 6,820 died. Although more than 1,000 Japanese were taken prisoner about 20,000 died in the fighting. According to the Iwo Jima veterans association, about one third of all Marines killed in action in World War II died at Iwo Jima before the island was secured on 26 March. More than 130 of those who died were never identified.

The figures seem alarmingly high, particularly bearing in mind the small size of the island, but there is a coda to this action that makes for better accounting. After Iwo Jima was in American hands some 30,000 US airmen made emergency landings there after getting into difficulties during bombing raids on Japan. Without the facility at Iwo Jima the presumption is that those men would have lost their lives or at least been casualties in the conflict.

Twenty seven Congressional Medals of Honor were awarded following the struggle for the island, more than were awarded to the Marines and the navy in any other

battle in US history. And while great exploits were often marked with a medal, many other acts of bravery and valour went unsung. By now the definitions by which the range of medals available to serving men were awarded began to appear arbitrary and that reduced the general respect for them.

Iwo Jima was administered by the US until 1968, when it was returned to the Japanese government. By that time the bodies of the Marines buried there had been returned to America.

The trauma was great but for the US Marines worse was to follow. The next step was deemed to be Okinawa in the Ryukyu Islands, sitting snugly in Japan's own backyard.

Assault on Okinawa

The participants of Operation *Iceberg* didn't know it but this was to be the largest major battle of the war. It began on 26 March 1945 when small islands off Okinawa were seized to act as forward bases in the campaign. The amphibious

Marine Rockets

American Marine Corps rocketeers attack Japanese positions in Iwo Jima in support of an advance.

Kamikaze Strike

Looking aft on the flight deck of the aircraft carrier Bunker Hill, *while her crew fight fires caused by Kamikaze hits off Okinawa, 11 May 1945*

assault opened on Easter Sunday, 1 April, and fighting lasted until June.

Earmarked for the assault were the men of the newly formed Tenth US Army, commanded by Lieutenant General Simon Bolivar Buckner. The aim at the time was still to mount an invasion of Japan proper and Okinawa would be an essential air base for just such an operation. The island was the biggest of the chain but nevertheless still only measured 66 miles long and was nowhere bigger than 10 miles in width.

Gathering in the region was the largest number of ships ever involved in a Pacific operation, numbering nearly 1,500. The Allied manpower levels were approaching half a million.

Once again, the initial landings, following the by now established pattern of a preliminary aerial bombardment, were

unexpectedly quiet. It wasn't until the first few days of the campaign had elapsed that it became clear the Japanese garrison was holed up in the south of the island in the vicinity of the capital

Now the attacks by Kamikaze were in earnest. Some 25 American ships were sunk and 165 others were damaged as loyal Japanese fliers made the final sacrifice.

There appears to have been a plan to send the mighty battleship *Yamato* on a suicide mission to Okinawa, taking out as many of the American ships in the vicinity as possible before succumbing to enemy firepower. She was stopped 200 miles short of her destination after being spotted by both US submarines and carrier reconnaissance aircraft.

On 7 April fliers from Task Force 58 inflicted as much damage as they were able

and eventually the last lady of the once-great Japanese fleet rolled over and sank, taking almost all hands with her. Other suicide boats on a lesser scale did their utmost to destablize the Allied fleet, with limited success.

On land the defenders were equally desperate. Joining the ranks of 77,000 troops of the Thirty-Second Japanese Army were men, women and children of the island's militia, fearful of their fate at the hands of the Americans. Once again the defenders fell back to a cave system that was largely impervious to bombardment from air and sea.

Before the battle was many days old a stalemate developed. No matter what the Americans threw at the Japanese defensive lines – known as the Shuri line for an ancient castle nearby – they proved impossible to breach. On 11 May Buckner orchestrated an all-out assault to shred the opposition. It failed and the wearying war of attrition went on

Into the Caves

Marines await the result of a grenade tossed into a Japanese cave position on Okinawa, April 1945.

Airstrikes

Japanese Kamikaze pilots attacking elements of a US Navy carrier task force off Okinawa, March 1945.

Last Defenders

US troops use a ladder to cross a gulch on Okinawa as they mop up the last resistance from the Japanese defenders.

along the same lines as before.

At the end of May the Japanese decided on a withdrawal to more southerly positions. Any hopes the Americans had of ploughing through the lines at this stage were thwarted partly by a fanatical defence and partly by abominable weather conditions.

The Pyschological Warfare Branch of the US Army Force stepped in with a leaflet designed to convince the Japanese of the merit of surrender:

Your wounded cannot get even enough medical care and day and night your men are falling all about you. They are indeed in a pitiable condition.
After seeing these sad things do you get carried away by a temporary emotional hot-

bloodedness, show true love for your men by forcing them to die a dog's death. Is this the best plan?
Look at the example of Germany where because the officers gave their full consent a million valuable lives were saved in order to build a newly living nation after the war... we urge that you officers who are responsible for the care of the men of your command, should act with prudence and decision.'

One of many such leaflets carefully crafted to appeal especially to the Japanese and written in their native tongue, it was scattered over the remaining forces but registered no effect.

Even when the Japanese soldiers were encircled in three pockets, their position hopeless, surrender was not on the cards. Buckner made an appeal to the Japanese commander on Okinawa, Lieutenant General Mitsuri Ushijima, imploring him to surrender to save the lives of the remaining troops. Still Ushijima fought on for another full week before committing suicide on 23 June. Prior to his death he sent a report to Tokyo: 'Our strategy, tactics and equipment were used to the utmost and we fought valiantly, but it was nothing before the material might of the enemy.'

In the battle for Okinawa there were some notable casualties, including Buckner, hit by shell fragments one day after making his appeal to the Japanese to surrender, one of the senior ranking victims of the entire conflict. Perhaps more famous still was war correspondent Ernie Taylor Pyle who died in a hail of machine gun bullets. He was a roving correspondent whose column was syndicated to about 200 newspapers in America. His authority and expertise was such that in 1944 he won the Pulitzer Prize. In the same year he earned immense popularity among the troops for pressing the case that soldiers in combat should get 'fight' pay just as airmen received 'flight' pay. Congress adopted his suggestion and it became law shortly before his death.

Surrender

Wounded Japanese defender on Okinawa emerges from a bunker to surrender to watchful US troops.

CHAPTER FOURTEEN

Little Boy and Fat Man: Using the Atom Bomb

After Okinawa, the US estimated that to take the Japanese home islands would cost a million casualties; this estimate played a major part in the decision to use the atomic bomb against Japan.

The Big Three at Potsdam

Marshal Josef Stalin, Prime Minister Winston Churchill and President Truman with their staffs around the conference table at Potsdam, July 1945.

By the spring of 1945 Japan was beaten in the war of the Pacific. Even its rulers realized the empire was in a no-win situation yet still there was procrastination among leading Japanese statesmen as an honourable exit to the conflict was sought.

The Allies therefore could not shift from their main aim, to obliterate Japan's ability to wage war. The task weighed heavily as the cost to the Allied armies – particularly that of the US – would be great. Just as loyal Germans had fought on the streets of Berlin during the dying hours of the Third Reich, so the Japanese reserves would surely battle long and hard to defend the heart of the empire from invasion. Some 5,300 aircraft had been hoarded on the home islands to carry out Kamikaze attacks. An increasing use of suicide boats was likely as some 3,300 were being packed with explosives to greet American shipping.

Nonetheless, plans were prepared for the invasion of the home islands involving as many as five million Allied troops. Operation *Olympic*, the codename given to an attack on Kyushu, was scheduled to begin on 1 October 1945. A second operation known as *Coronet* would deliver the final blow in the early months of the following year. Once the war in Europe was over there would be manpower a plenty to carry out the task. Yet the picture in the Far East was not yet clear cut.

The British were making progress through south-east Asia but the job was not yet done. The requirement for them to provide aerial and naval support might be

compromised as the fighting continued. Americans were still involved in fighting on the Philippines that proved a distraction to the task in hand. The customary three-way wrangle between the US army, navy and marine corps began to rear its head again as planners pondered the most likely way to force a Japanese surrender.

Another consideration was the arrival in the Allied corral of Stalin and his sizeable Soviet forces. His stated aim had always been to defeat Hitler before engaging on another front. Now Stalin had an eye for territorial gain in the Pacific at the expense of its old enemy, Japan, and was poised to begin hostilities. America and Britain, however, were wary about the aspirations of the Soviet leader.

In April 1945 Roosevelt died in office and Harry Truman became president. He ordered another review of the invasion plans, anxious to preserve American lives as best he could yet not wishing to compromise on the desire for unconditional surrender by Japan.

A Question of Honour

With the odds stacked against her, would Japan surrender? Many of her cities were already in ruins thanks to the ceaseless B-29 strategic bombing. The submarine blockade had deprived the islands of those commodities necessary to continue the battle. Kamikaze planes would not be able to get off the ground without fuel so their potency would quickly be knocked out. Indeed, the army and defiant civilians could not fight without food. Shortages in Japan were already chronic in the early months of 1945. Some top ranking generals believed that capitulation was only a matter of time, even that the estimates for Allied casualties had been hopelessly inflated.

All the while there was another element as yet in the experimental stages. It

Enola Gay

the US B-29 bomber which dropped the first atomic bomb on Hiroshima during World War II, now at Roswell Army Airfield in New Mexico.

was, of course, the atom bomb, being developed on behalf of the US and Britain in secrecy at Los Alamo, New Mexico, under the supervision of scientist Robert Oppenheimer.

The whole conflict had been characterized by mighty leaps in technology. The aircraft that took to the skies in 1941 when war broke out between Japan and the US now possessed better weapons, could fly for longer, would land on ever shorter runways. Radar (the acronym for radio detection and ranging) – in its infancy in the late thirties – was now fitted as standard to ships, submarines and aircraft. The bazooka was just one of the weapons created as the conflict continued. Amphibious warfare, both in terms of the equipment used and its conduct, had advanced beyond recognition. Yet the atomic bomb was something apart from these, something new era that was at once awesome and awful.

Its creation had been considered as early as 1904 following initial experiments revealing the intense energy expended by radioactive atoms. Thereafter physicists across the globe worked on the possibilities thrown up by nuclear fusion and fission. Paradoxically, the Allied cause was aided by Hitler himself when he purged Jews from German society. Some remarkable scientific talents were given shelter by Britain and later America and they worked tirelessly to bring the bomb project to fruition. (Germany's equivalent programme was way behind, as observers after the European war noted.)

The exercise is remembered as a predominantly American affair and indeed in its later stages the US dominated. However, its early impetus came from or via Britain. Lieutenant Colonel Leslie R. Groves, who was at the head of the Manhattan Project from September 1942 following his successful completion of the Pentagon building, once wrote: 'Prime Minister Churchill was probably the best friend that the Manhattan Project ever had.'

Churchill gave his consent for the bomb to be used against Japan as early as 4 July, before the trial had even taken place. He later gave his reasons for doing so. 'To avert a vast, indefinite butchery, to bring the war to an end, to give peace to the world, to lay healing hands upon its tortured peoples by a manifestation of overwhelming power at the cost of a few explosions, seemed, after all our toils and perils, the miracle of development.'

The first plutonium bomb detonation occurred at Alamogordo on 16 July 1945. The following day the Potsdam conference began. At the conference Truman got word of the successful atomic bomb trial and finally confided its existence to Stalin. Of course, the irascible tyrant already knew all about the bomb thanks to sympathetic surveillance. His own bomb project was well underway although the official secrecy surrounding the Manhattan Project convinced him that Soviet Russia would be left out in the cold by America and Britain when hostilities ceased. Still scheming to secure the best position for Soviet Russia he spoke in brief and vague terms about Japanese entreaties made to his envoys and ambassadors, declining to mention that messages intimating a possible peace deal had come from the highest level. His thoughts were not with the people of Japan but with how much of that country he could scythe off for himself.

Meanwhile Truman was looking for ways to counterbalance the mushrooming Soviet power base. Indeed, as Soviet help

Atomic Cloud

The infamous mushroom cloud of the atomic bomb explosion over Hiroshima, 6 August 1945. Although this image has become a symbol of the horrors of nuclear war, more people died in conventional bombing on this same day.

City in Dust

Allied officers look out over the ruins of Hiroshima after the dropping of the atom bomb.

was no longer needed to quell the Japanese, Truman was more robust in the denial of Stalin's demands at that conference than any leader had been before. Truman knew he had direct control of a weapon that not only would end the war, but would help put the control of post-war politics in his hands.

Dropping Little Boy

Almost before the dust settled from the trial, the first uranium bomb, nicknamed 'Little Boy', was being loaded onto the USS *Indianapolis* in San Fransisco – a ship that had just undergone repairs to damage caused by a Kamikaze at Okinawa. A canister containing the bomb was welded to the deck for the long journey to Tinian. After leaving American shores on 16 July

it took ten days to complete the journey to its Pacific destination.

No one on board except for a select few knew the nature of the cargo. The disaster that might have been soon became starkly apparent. Three days after the bomb was taken off the ship it was torpedoed as it made its way to the Philippines for training exercises, by a Japanese submarine. The ship sank in just twelve minutes, apparently leaving no time to send an SOS, although it now appears probable that one was in fact sent, but ignored as a Japanese trick. Of the almost 1,200 men on the ship, around 300 went down with her. The remaining 900 were left in the shark-infested waters of the Philippine Sea for over three days until being spotted by a passing flying-boat, which took some of the survivors on board and radioed an SOS. When the remaining survivors were picked up by the USS *Cecil Doyle*, there were just 319 left alive.

On 6 August Operation *Centreboard* swung into action. Early in the morning a USAF B-29 called *Enola Gay* bearing the atomic bomb, under the command of Colonel Tibbets, took off from Tinian. Some hours later the fearsome weapon, producing a blast equivalent to 20,000 tons of TNT, was unleashed above Hiroshima. Everything in a two-mile radius of the explosion's epicentre was vaporized. The subsequent inferno was so immense that a tail gunner on *Enola Gay* exclaimed: 'My God, what have we done?'

Another crew member, Sgt George Caron, described the deadly mushroom cloud he saw forming behind him: 'It's like a mass of bubbling molasses. The mushroom is spreading out. It's maybe a mile or two wide and half a mile high. It's growing up and up. It's nearly level with us and climbing. It's very black but there is a purplish tint to the cloud. The base of the mushroom looks like a heavy undercast that is shot through with flames.'

In an instant the death toll was an estimated 78,000. Thousands more were injured as the shock wave spread across the city, shortly followed by a firestorm and many of those would die from their horrific wounds. The devastating effects of radiation were felt for years to come. A city of 90,000 buildings was reduced to just 28,000 while the shape of warfare was change forever. There was no distinction between military and civilian targets. All were swept to their deaths by a deadly nuclear wind, just as the scientists, military and politicians knew they would be.

From the Allied point of view the unconditional surrender they required was still not forthcoming. As if to make a mark of its own, Soviet Russia declared war on Japan on 8 August. The following day a second atomic bomb was dropped from a B-29 called *Bockscar* on Nagasaki, where about 39,000 people were killed. Japan could not sustain any further relentless retribution by the Allies.

The following day, after late night crisis talks in the cabinet, the Japanese accepted surrender terms 'on the understanding that it does not comprise any demand which prejudices the prerogatives of the emperor as sovereign ruler.'

CHAPTER FIFTEEN

Surrender

After Okinawa, the US estimated that to take the Japanese home islands would cost a million casualties; this estimate played a major part in the decision to use the atomic bomb against Japan.

Freedom

Allied prisoners of war celebrating their liberation from Changi Jail, Singapore. The extreme harshness with which Japan treated prisoners of war was only fully realized after the liberation.

In typically Japanese style the empire's loyal subjects had gone off to war in 1941 with unrealistically inflated views on their own ability to win.

Troops departing from Japan in the heady days of December 1941 were given a booklet to enlighten them as to the nature of their enemies:

'Westerners – being very superior people, very effeminate and very cowardly – have an intense dislike of fighting in the rain or the mist or at night. Night in particular (although it is excellent for dancing), they cannot conceive to be a proper time for war. In this, if we seize upon it, lies our great opportunity.'

Later, in a pamphlet called 'The Psychology of the Individual American' distributed to Japanese troops they learned still more about the Americans:

They are expert liars, they are taken in by flattery and propaganda. Their desires are very materialistic. They go into battle with no spiritual incentive, and rely on material superiority.

But the dream of the clumsily titled Great East Asia Coprosperity Sphere, a blueprint for the way Japan saw the model existence of its corner of the globe, now lay in tatters. Their moral claim to a new world order was smashed to smithereens.

As far as military matters went, the navy proved it was not invincible, the army could be beaten despite the tenacity of its soldiers, and many of its strategies were found wanting. Night fighting had proved effective and, at first, good use was made of the superior Zero aircraft. But the Japanese did not capitalize on initial air superiority nor did it thoroughly grasp the advantages of it. Every soldier, sailor and citizen committed 100 per cent to the conflict but it was all for nought.

As one the Japanese population on the home islands, in prison camps, in hiding in the occupied territories, bowed their heads when they heard the emperor broadcast to his subjects on 14 August.

He told his people they must 'endure the unendurable and suffer the insufferable'. He was not talking about the after effects of the atomic bomb but of surrender. Even now some in his regime harboured hopes of an honourable defeat and stormed the emperor's palace in a bid to halt the process of surrender. They were beaten back by the emperor's loyal guard.

V(ictory) J(apan) day was declared as 15 August, with celebrations being held worldwide. Some of the most heartfelt celebrations were among the American citizens of Japanese extraction who had been locked up behind barbed wire in internment camps at the outbreak of war, as a threat to national security.

Pockets of Japanese resistance in far flung corners of the empire Japan had once called its own gave up piecemeal.

On 2 September Japanese representative Mamoru Shigemitsu, the one-legged foreign minister clad in top hat and tails, signed the surrender on board the battleship USS *Missouri* in Tokyo Bay. General MacArthur was asked by one of his aides: 'Are you going to call on the emperor?'

'No,' he replied. 'The emperor will come to me.'

It's Over

Signing the documents of surrender aboard the USS Missouri, *2 September 1945, ending the Second World War.*

And a few days later he did. He told MacArthur: 'I come to you...to offer myself to the judgement of the powers you represent as the one who bears sole responsibility for every political and military decision made and action taken by my people in the conduct of the war.'

He was not, however, charged as a war criminal, an issue that would cause controversy for years afterwards. The Emperor's divine status amongst the Japanese people was never fully grasped by the Allies as, without him wishing it, the war was for months continued on his behalf. But they deemed it likely that armed insurrection would occur if the position of emperor was compromised.

For their part the Americans had limited understanding of the Japanese state of mind. The desire for a 'no strings' surrender was perpetually emphasized by the Allies, who were anxious that there were no rallying points left over upon which the cause for another war could be pegged in the near future. Until the Japanese would talk the talk of unconditional surrender, the Allies refused to halt their war efforts, imposing a glass ceiling on events. Yet there were numerous indications that a compromise could be reached with a little open-minded thinking.

Culturally, it was clear the Japanese would never surrender if they believed the fate of the emperor was at stake. Hence they held on into hopelessness for the love of their ruler. When defeat was staring them in the face they spoke about giving up the fight if the safety of 'his majesty' could be guaranteed. Had the Allies been fully aware of the diplomatically-worded messages coming out of Japan differently the war might have ended sooner.

Alas, the Japanese prime minister Suzuki made a catastrophic mistake in choosing Soviet Russia as the 'neutral' country that might help negotiate a peace. The armistice feelers were never picked up where it mattered, among the American top brass.

The shame of being branded a war criminal cut deep for numerous Japanese leaders, many whom chose to commit suicide. Before his execution Tojo made clear his position on the war:

Never at any time did I conceive that the waging of this war would or could be challenged by the victors as an international crime or that regularly constituted officials of the vanquished nations would be charged individually as criminals under any recognized international law or under alleged violations of treaties between nations. I feel that I did no wrong. I feel that I did what was right and true.

With hindsight the scapegoat nature of the post-war trials appears starkly apparent. They were orchestrated at a time when the Allies knew the Japanese to be brutal fighters, guilty of shocking savagery. They were by turns capable of beating sick and wounded men and disembowelling women and children. Famously they beheaded prisoners of war with one swing of a sword. But these are broad brush strokes that highlight only the most barbaric of Japanese fighters and pay no regard to cultural gulfs between the two sides. There were numerous others who fought in the same manner as other soldiers around the globe during the era. Many of their number passed the dull hours between actions writing Tanka, traditional five line poems that were both lyrical and moving.

Intelligence reports based on interroga-

Jubilation

Crowds gathering in Times Square to read the news of Japan's surrender on V-J (Victory Japan) Day, New York City.

tion of prisoners captured during Allied attacks on Japanese-held islands in early May 1945 revealed still more about the serving soldier, most of whom were conscripted men.

The reports suggest that morale was generally low among Japanese troops, particularly the conscripts. Most of the latter were ageing, ill-equipped, in poor health and with barely a month's training were no match for the advancing Allies. They appeared to particularly resent the superior attitude and arrogance of regular Japanese soldiers, NCOs and officers.

Prisoner PW X3004 Konno Kleichi, a 30-year-old farmer captured north of Omanay on May 2, had been unable to keep up with his unit's retreat – hardly surprising given the debilitating effects of malaria. The interrogating officer, Squadron Leader F W Clifton of the Royal Australian Air Force, noted that:

Morale of troops in PW's (prisoner of war's) unit was very low. All of the 120 men in the unit, except three or four, were ill at various times with malaria. C.O. of the Unit, 1st Lieutenant Togashi, addressed the men on 29th April 45 and told them that there was nothing left for them to do but swallow their pride and retreat.

Under REMARKS Clifton adds:

PW had received little military training and had not fired his rifle on this island.

Another of Clifton's interviewees, PW X2011 Sadayoshi Tenga, a 30-year-old fish market owner serving as a Private First Class with the 165th II Battalion, 75th Bdo, was captured on Samal island on 8 May. He said he'd deserted to anti-Japanese guerrilla forces because he was 'disgusted with ill treatment received from army officers and NCOs.' Tenga believed that, for the same reason, many conscripts had deserted on Mindano and had 'gone to the mountains'. He told Clifton:

The attitude of the regular soldiers to the newly-conscripted men was that of contempt. PW was often ill-treated by officers and men.

Another interrogation report reveals the nobility of one Major Matsuzaki in the Philippines when dealing with a young woman with a Japanese father and the Filipino mother who had been guilty of spying for the Americans. Clearly, they had previously developed a father-daughter relationship that came into play when the convicted woman requested that the major carried out her execution. The date was deferred by a day as it was the Emperor's birthday and, that night, the major negotiated her escape to Samal Island. She survived to be interrogated closely by a squadron leader in the Royal Australian Air Force as early as May 1945. The fate of the major is unknown.

On 10 September 1945 Briton R. Munby was posted to Singapore to help oversee the transition of power from the vanquished to the victors. Shortly before his arrival 300 Japanese officers committed hari kiri or ritual suicide in the lounge of the Raffles Hotel. A whole platoon of officers blew themselves up with hand grenades:

The Chinese in Chinatown were much happier to see the British than the Malayans. Everywhere there I was met with pleasant faces and words of thanks though many of the poorer people were so near to starvation point that it ust have been indeed an effort for them even to smile. The very fact that I saw a dead woman dressed in the black smock of the working class, lying in the gutter, most conspicuous but completelyunheeded by passers-by pointed conclusviely to the fact that such bodies were a common sight during the Japanese reign of terror.'

He watched as Japanese prisoners were marched to the YMCA building – previously the headquarters of the Kempei, the notorious Japanese secret police:

'The Japs passed within three feet of where I was standing and it was interesting to note the expressions on their faces. Some showed signs of great humiliation and were probably unwilling tools forced to carry out their government's orders; others were arrogant, brutal creatures to whom the catcalls and derision of the crowd meant not a thing.'

The official surrender of Singapore came on 12 September and was made to Mountbatten. As Japanese money was immediately scrapped cigarettes became currency. There followed a period of chaos and confusion through which only one thing was entirely clear, that the days of British rule in Singapore were limited, as they were in other colonial possessions. The Japanese dream – to see Europeans ousted from Asia – would inevitably come to pass. Alas, there remained several decades before the dream became a reality as America and Europe wrestled with the concept that Asians were fully able to govern themselves.

With armed conflict raging in Asia throughout the fifties and sixties it seems the fond hopes held by the Americans and British of obliterating future causes of war ultimately came to nothing. In some way lost fighter Hiroo Onada could count himself lucky. He emerged from the jungle of Lubang Islands in the Philippines still armed with a rifle and hand grenades on 9 March 1974, one of numerous soldiers who refused to believe the fight had finished. He surrendered some 29 years after the Japanese hierarchy, having entirely missed some of the worst excesses of warfare known to man.

Index